BUILD A SIMPLE DINGHY

BUILD A SIMPLE DINGHY

Ian Nicolson
Alasdair Reynolds

ADLARD COLES LIMITED
8 Grafton Street, London W1

Adlard Coles Ltd
William Collins Sons & Co. Ltd
8 Grafton Street, London W1X 3LA

First published in Great Britain by
Adlard Coles Ltd 1987

Distributed in the United States of America
by Sheridan House, Inc.

British Library Cataloguing in Publication Data

Nicolson, Ian
  Build a simple dinghy.
  1. Sailboats 2. Boat-building—Amateurs'
  manuals
  I. Title II. Reynolds, Alasdair
  623.8'223   VM351

ISBN 0-229-11806-2

Photoset by Deltatype, Ellesmere Port
Printed and bound in Great Britain by
R. J. Acford, Chichester

While all the designs in this book have been built and
found satisfactory in practice, no liability is accepted
by the authors or publishers in respect of any boat
which anyone may build or attempt to build to these
designs. When going afloat, do not set out until the
weather forecast has been checked, always wear a
life-jacket, and beginners should sail in company.

To Christopher and Campbell Reynolds
In thanks for a thousand hours spent turning boats over in bitter cold basements, photographing half-built hulls in dimly-lit sheds, carrying dinghies from building base to the shore through deep snow, launching craft off gale-wracked beaches, worrying about small boats in horrid seas without saying too much, taking out our newly-built boats on trials and making helpful suggestions, typing manuscripts without commenting on unusual spelling, providing the unlimited tea and home-made cakes which are essential for any boat-building project, and a thousand other things.

Contents

CHAPTER 1
Boatbuilding is easy

Before you picked up this book you may have thought boatbuilding was best left to professionals or, at the very least, experienced amateurs. This is not the case. Boatbuilding can be simple and, apart from enabling you to get afloat as cheaply as possible, it is a rewarding hobby in itself.

Ian is a professional with many years' experience of designing and building boats behind him. Many of his previous books have been written with the amateur builder in mind. Up until the time that the authors got together to build *Cove Boat*, Alasdair's woodworking experience extended to simple household items made in carpentry lessons at school. The sequence of boatbuilding projects starting with *Cove Boat*, progressing to *Longa* and then *Kilda*, followed a learning curve from an amateur's point of view.

With *Cove Boat* and *Longa* all that is needed is familiarity with the use of simple hand tools. We have provided all the information necessary to

Plan 1.1 All the boats in this book can be built in a bedroom. Provided, that is, the hull when complete can be carried out through the door or window. Make up a rough pattern and try this operation before starting to build the boat in a room. Maybe a garage, warehouse, boatyard, empty shop, church hall, school building, unused factory, basement or loft would be better. If the worst comes to the worst, build a temporary shelter using plastic sheeting and a wooden framework.

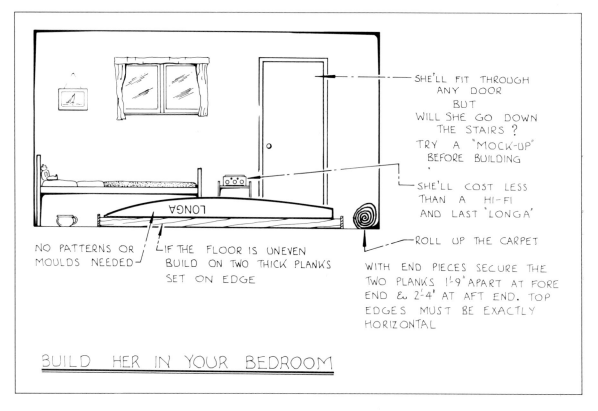

SHE'LL FIT THROUGH ANY DOOR
BUT
WILL SHE GO DOWN THE STAIRS ?
TRY A "MOCK-UP" BEFORE BUILDING

SHE'LL COST LESS THAN A HI-FI AND LAST 'LONGA'

ROLL UP THE CARPET

NO PATTERNS OR MOULDS NEEDED

IF THE FLOOR IS UNEVEN BUILD ON TWO THICK PLANKS SET ON EDGE

WITH END PIECES SECURE THE TWO PLANKS 1'-9" APART AT FORE END & 2'-4' AT AFT END. TOP EDGES MUST BE EXACTLY HORIZONTAL

BUILD HER IN YOUR BEDROOM

build *Cove Boat* and *Longa* in this book. *Kilda* makes an excellent project for those with a little previous experience. The construction of *Kilda* is described in detail; however, it is difficult to reproduce drawings for a boat of this type at an adequate scale in a book, so large drawings can be purchased from the authors.

Punto and *Beachboat* were designed and built by a friend, David Ryder-Turner. We are pleased to be able to include descriptions of these boats which add to the variety of simple craft in this book. Plans and instructions for them can be obtained from him at the address given in those chapters.

If you already have a dinghy there are ideas here which are useful for repairs and improvements.

All the boats in the book can be built in a normal room, but check that the completed boat can be carried out of the room and out of the house. Do this by making a disposable pattern or dummy from cardboard held together with Sellotape and staples. Better still, make up a crude shape out of scrap wood nailed together. Use these dummies to make sure the final boat will fit on your car and stow in your garage.

When buying wood for constructing these boats, go for good-quality wood free from knots, cracks and blemishes. Screws should be brass, bronze or stainless steel; never use mild steel fastenings.

We recommend the use of two-part epoxy glue for constructing these boats, which we obtained from Structural Polymer Systems Ltd, Love Lane, Cowes, Isle of Wight, England, PO31 7EV (Tel: 0983 298451). Follow the manufacturer's instructions for the use of the glue and observe their health and safety recommendations. We found that S.P. Systems were always happy to discuss the likely quantities and application of their product which can be obtained direct from them or from local distributors in some areas. Where excess glue has been used, it should be wiped off with a rag before it hardens. Where glue has to be faired off, this should be done when the glue has set to the consistency of a very hard cheese and before it becomes rock solid.

When interpreting and reading plans it is sometimes necessary to mark 'offsets' in order to achieve the required shape of a particular part of the boat. In Chapter 2 on *Cove Boat*, section 1 of 'Building notes' contains a detailed description of this process which readers may find useful generally.

The following is a fairly comprehensive list of tools for building these boats (they are not all required for the simpler ones):

Handsaw (10 teeth per inch)	Surform
Tenon saw (14 teeth per inch)	Rat-tail file (round in section)
Small hammer (6 oz)	Bevel gauge
Two screwdrivers ($\frac{1}{4}$ in and $\frac{3}{8}$ in)	Work-bench with vice

Hand drill and bits ($\frac{1}{16}$–$\frac{1}{4}$ in), plus countersink
Tape measure
2 ft rule
Set square
Clamps (jaws 4 in and 8 in)
Plane
Chalk and pencils
Paint brushes ($\frac{1}{2}$ in and 1 in)
Clean jam jars, plastic boxes or tubs for glue
Glue applicators (can be pieces of wood $10 \times \frac{3}{4} \times \frac{1}{8}$ in)

In addition, an electric drill and an electric jigsaw make life easier and building quicker.

The ideas and drawings in this book can be used to build a variety of boats, not just those detailed here.

CHAPTER 2
Cove Boat 8 feet 3 inches overall

Cove Boat is so simple and cheap, children can build her. She offers amazing scope for her small size. She is suitable for two children or one adult. She is stable and, being fully decked, is ideal for learning to sail. She can be carried easily on top of a small car. With a very small outboard on the transom, she can even be used for fishing. *Cove Boat* is adaptable and fun, and must be the most uncomplicated boat ever devised.

It all started at a party. The authors were chatting about boats. Alasdair mentioned that he was looking for a little boat that could be used for sailing or fishing and would be easy to carry on top of a car. Ian said that he had an idea which he had already sketched out that might fit the bill. We subsequently got together to look at the idea. *Cove Boat* was born and our boatbuilding partnership began!

Cove Boat is so simple that, until they saw the boat on the water, some

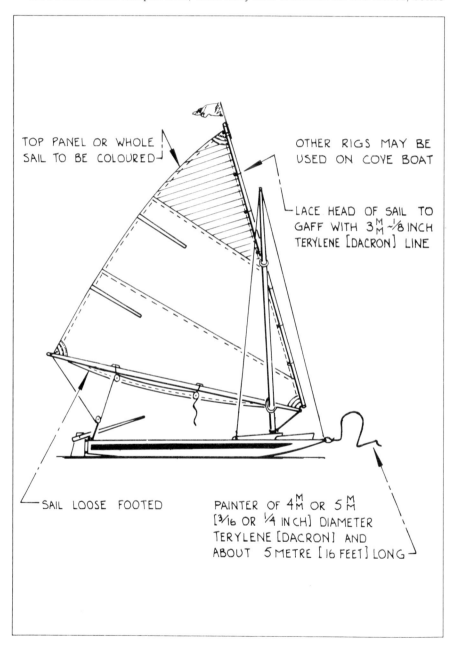

TOP PANEL OR WHOLE
SAIL TO BE COLOURED

OTHER RIGS MAY BE
USED ON COVE BOAT

LACE HEAD OF SAIL TO
GAFF WITH 3^M_M ~$\frac{1}{8}$ INCH
TERYLENE [DACRON] LINE

SAIL LOOSE FOOTED

PAINTER OF 4^M_M OR 5^M_M
[$\frac{3}{16}$ OR $\frac{1}{4}$ INCH] DIAMETER
TERYLENE [DACRON] AND
ABOUT 5 METRE [16 FEET] LONG

Plan 2.1 Sail plan.
Sail dimensions are:
Normal rig
Luff 9 ft 8 in
Foot 8 ft 9 in
Leech 9 ft 5 in

Large rig
Luff 10 ft 8 in
Foot 8 ft 9 in
Leech 10 ft

Spar lengths are:
Normal rig
Mast 8 ft 6 in
Gaff 10 ft
Boom 9 ft

Large rig
Mast 9 ft 6 in
Gaff 11 ft
Boom 9 ft

people thought she would not work. They ate their words when they took her for a sail. She is a remarkably attractive and endearing little craft. She performs well and is great fun whilst being an ideal boat for learning to sail.

Careful study of the plans and notes that follow provides all the information necessary to build the boat. All the materials are easily obtainable.

▶ COVE BOAT – WOOD REQUIREMENTS

1. Two sheets 8 ft × 4 ft marine plywood 4 mm thick. Make sure each ply sheet is *fully* 8 ft × 4 ft *before* accepting delivery or beginning construction. One sheet can be of varnishing grade for the deck if you prefer and the other of painting grade.
2. Eight pieces white pine 8 ft 6 in × 8 in × $\frac{3}{4}$ in planed all over.
3. Three pieces white pine 10 ft 3 in × 2 in × 2 in. These can be unplaned. If you have chosen the larger rig, one of these pieces will need to be 11 ft 3 in long (3 in longer than the plan, to allow for trimming and finishing).
4. Two pieces white pine 8 ft 6 in × 1 in × $\frac{3}{8}$ in planed all over.

The pine should have as few knots as possible (particularly the 10 ft 3 in pieces) and any unavoidable knots should *not* be loose and should not run right through the thickness of the wood.

▶ COVE BOAT – BUILDING NOTES

Please read these notes right through before commencing construction. You will be able to save time and material by carrying out gluing or varnishing of certain components in batches.

All screws used should be made of brass, bronze or stainless steel. We used 2-part epoxy glue produced by Structural Polymer Systems Ltd. A metric conversion table is on page 101.

1·Cutting out the sides

(a) Select the two best 8 ft 6 in planks (see 2 above), with as few knots as possible. There should be *no* knots in line with the top and bottom edges or ends.

(b) Mark off 12 in intervals on one of the planks.

(c) Mark 'offsets' which are the widths of the side (as shown on plan 2.3) every 12 in. Start at the $1\frac{1}{8}$ in width which is the bow.

(d) Join up the marks into a 'fair line' using a thin wooden batten, drawing a pencil line along the batten.

(e) Cut along $\frac{1}{16}$ in outside the fair line and plane the edge smooth. Remember to plane from the centre to the ends to suit the grain.

(f) Lay down the side you have just cut on your other best plank. Use the first side as a pattern for the second side. Mark the second plank, again leaving $\frac{1}{16}$ in all round for finishing. Cut it to shape and plane the edge smooth.

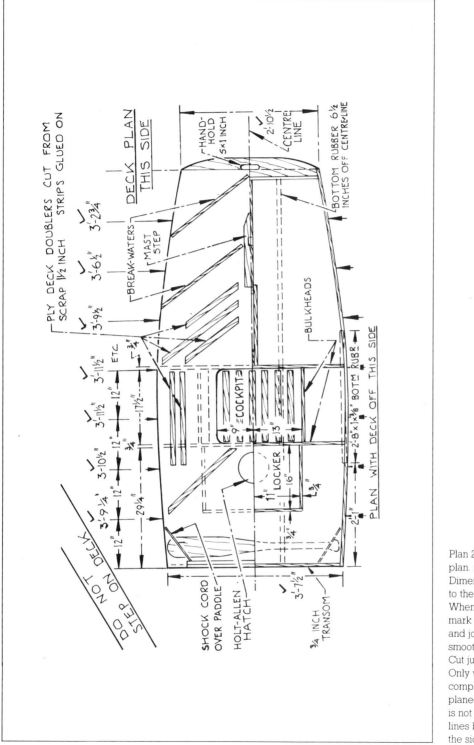

Plan 2.2 Hull and deck plan. IMPORTANT Dimensions marked ✓ are to the outside of the hull. When making the deck, mark off these dimensions and join up the marks with smooth fair pencil lines. Cut just outside the lines. Only when the hull is complete is the ply edge planed to size, and then it is not planed down to the lines but to the outside of the side planking.

7

Plan 2.3 Hull section.
IMPORTANT Dimensions
marked ✳ are from the
underside of the deck to
the top of the bottom ply.
This means that these
dimensions are the actual
height of the sides. When
making the sides, mark off
these dimensions on the
planks and join up the
marks with a fair curve.
Cut outside the pencil line
and plane down to it.
NOTE A Make two thus for
dagger-board casing from
¾ in solid wood.
NOTE B Bottom shape
matches curve of boat's
sides.
NOTE C Item VWZ is made
of solid wood ¾ in thick
and an identical shape
made from a ply offcut is
also needed.

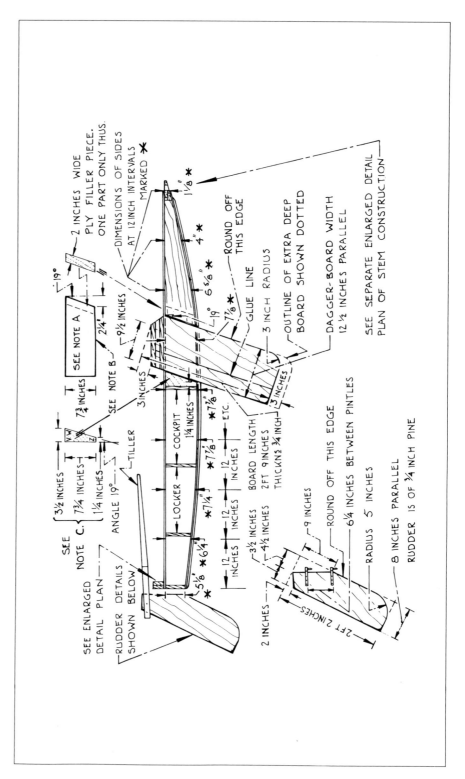

8

2·Cutting out the parts for the cockpit well/bulkhead framework

(a) Mark off and cut two pieces 3 ft 10 in × 8 in × ¾ in.

(b) Mark off and cut two pieces 1 ft 5½ in × 8 in × ¾ in. Mark the poorer sides of

items (a) 'cockpit ends' and items (b) 'cockpit sides'.

(c) Mark off and cut the three locker sides to the dimensions on plan 2.2.

3·Cutting out the rudder, tiller and dagger-board

(a) Mark off and cut one piece 2 ft 2 in × 8 in × ¾ in for rudder.

(b) Mark off and cut one piece 2 ft 9 in × 8 in × ¾ in for dagger-board.

(c) Mark off and cut one piece 2 ft 9 in × 4½ in × ¾ in for dagger-board.

(d) Mark off and cut strips as shown on plan 2.3 for the dagger-board hand-hold (plan 2.4).

Cut the rudder to shape as shown on plan 2.3 then bevel the edges (by planing and sandpapering) to give a more streamlined shape. Drill a hole in the rudder as shown on the plan for the tiller bolt.

Cut the dagger-board pieces to shape as shown on plan 2.3. Glue them together at the first gluing session (see below). They are glued edge to edge. The top strip is glued on one side for a handhold, and the second strip a bit lower (as shown on plan 2.4) to act as a stop to prevent the board going down too far.

For the tiller, cut a piece of pine or, if you prefer, hardwood 2 ft 2 in × 1½ in × ¾ in (allow a greater length of tiller as shown on plan 2.5 if desired). Cut two pieces of pine or hardwood 1 ft 2 in × 1½ in × ¾ in for the tiller side pieces (which clasp the rudder). Plane all the pieces smooth then taper the top and bottom of the tiller piece over the forward 6 in to form a comfortable handhold about 1 in × ¾ in as shown on plan 2.5. Taper the forward end of the two side pieces as shown on the plan then screw and glue them at the first gluing session (see below) as shown.

4·To make the sides bend

Make accurate ¼ in deep cuts across the inside of each side piece starting 1 ft from the bow then every 6 in as far as 4 ft back from the bow.

IMPORTANT **Choose the best faces for the *outsides* and cut port and starboard, ie make boards 'handed' – the cuts must be on the inside of whichever side (port or starboard) that you are working on. Mark the edges of the boards ¼ in across and stop the saw cuts at these marks.**

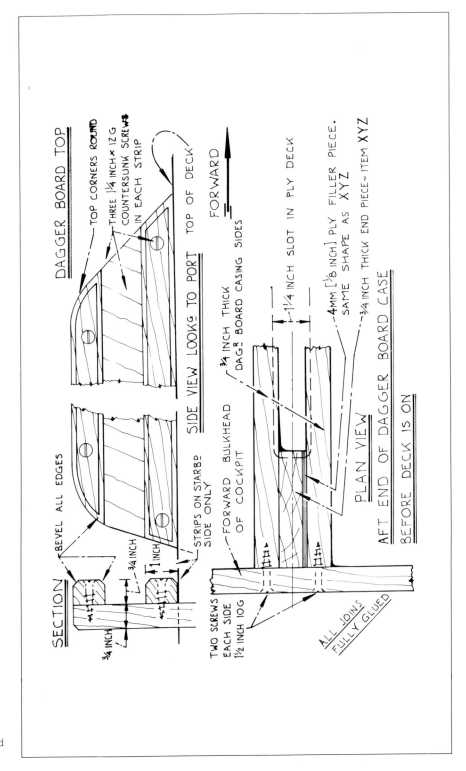

Plan 2.4 Dagger-board and dagger-board casing.

10

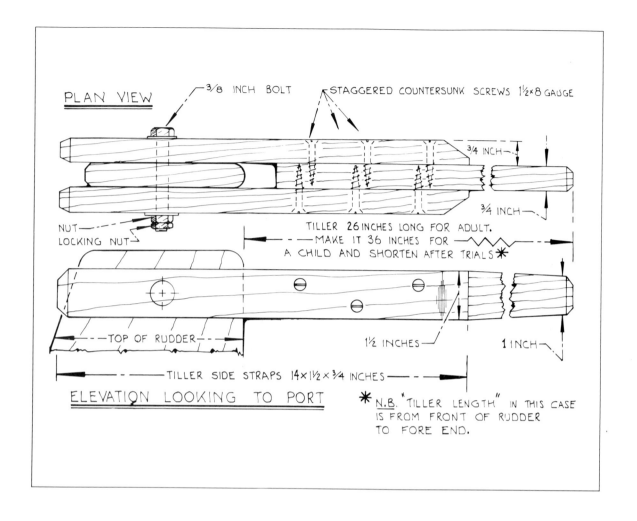

PLAN VIEW

3/8 INCH BOLT   STAGGERED COUNTERSUNK SCREWS 1½×8 GAUGE

3/4 INCH

3/4 INCH

NUT

LOCKING NUT

TILLER 26 INCHES LONG FOR ADULT.
MAKE IT 36 INCHES FOR
A CHILD AND SHORTEN AFTER TRIALS *

TOP OF RUDDER

1½ INCHES   1 INCH

TILLER SIDE STRAPS 14×1½×¾ INCHES

ELEVATION LOOKING TO PORT

* N.B. "TILLER LENGTH" IN THIS CASE
IS FROM FRONT OF RUDDER
TO FORE END.

5·Cutting out the transom and stem pieces

Plan 2.5 Tiller.

(a) Mark off and cut one piece 3 ft 6 in ×
     $5\frac{1}{8}$ in × $\frac{3}{4}$ in for the transom.

(b) Mark off and cut one piece 2 ft 9 in ×

(c) Mark off and cut one piece 2 ft 9 in ×
     $3\frac{3}{8}$ in × $\frac{3}{4}$ in for the stem.

$4\frac{1}{2}$ in × $\frac{3}{4}$ in for the stem.

Screw the stem pieces together with an overlap as shown on plan 2.6
and exactly in line, then bevel them by making a series of saw cuts
across the grain. Do *not* make the cuts too deep. The cuts should be
spaced about $1\frac{1}{2}$ in apart. Then chisel away surplus wood and plane
smooth accurately to the dimensions shown on plan 2.6.

Cut holes on either side fairly near the bottom of the transom for fitting
the bungs, and drill small holes either side to fit the bolts for securing the
bungs. Fit the lower rudder gudgeon with through bolts at the centre-
line of the transom so that the top of the gudgeon socket is situated 1 in
above the lower edge of the transom. (See plan 2.7.)

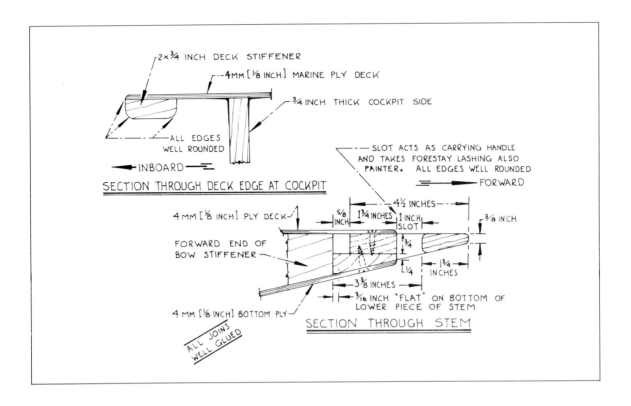

2×¾ INCH DECK STIFFENER

4MM [⅛ INCH] MARINE PLY DECK

¾ INCH THICK COCKPIT SIDE

ALL EDGES WELL ROUNDED

INBOARD

SECTION THROUGH DECK EDGE AT COCKPIT

SLOT ACTS AS CARRYING HANDLE AND TAKES FORESTAY LASHING ALSO PAINTER. ALL EDGES WELL ROUNDED

FORWARD

4MM [⅛ INCH] PLY DECK

FORWARD END OF BOW STIFFENER

4 MM [⅛ INCH] BOTTOM PLY

ALL JOINS WELL GLUED

⅝ INCH   1¾ INCHES   1 INCH SLOT

4½ INCHES

⅜ INCH

¾
¼

1¾ INCHES

3⅜ INCHES

3/16 INCH 'FLAT' ON BOTTOM OF LOWER PIECE OF STEM

SECTION THROUGH STEM

Plan 2.6 Cockpit edge and stem.

Plan 2.7 Transom and forward bulkhead. The bulkhead and a similar one aft form the ends of the cockpit.

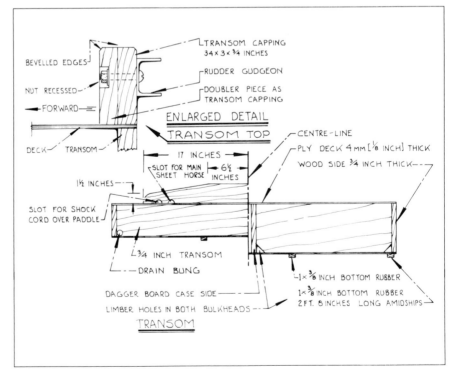

TRANSOM CAPPING 34 × 3 × ¾ INCHES

BEVELLED EDGES

RUDDER GUDGEON

DOUBLER PIECE AS TRANSOM CAPPING

NUT RECESSED

FORWARD

ENLARGED DETAIL TRANSOM TOP

DECK   TRANSOM

CENTRE-LINE

PLY DECK 4 MM [⅛ INCH] THICK

WOOD SIDE ¾ INCH THICK

17 INCHES

SLOT FOR MAIN SHEET HORSE

6½ INCHES

1½ INCHES

SLOT FOR SHOCK CORD OVER PADDLE

¾ INCH TRANSOM

DRAIN BUNG

DAGGER BOARD CASE SIDE

LIMBER HOLES IN BOTH BULKHEADS

1 × ⅜ INCH BOTTOM RUBBER

1 × ⅜ INCH BOTTOM RUBBER 2 FT. 8 INCHES LONG AMIDSHIPS

TRANSOM

6·Assembling the cockpit well/bulkhead framework

Mark the middle of the cockpit ends (see 2(a) above) then make marks 13 in to each side of the middle where the cockpit sides will be attached (see 2(b) above). Make the cockpit ends and sides fit well and then screw together with two screws at each join. Use $1\frac{1}{2}$ in screws and remember to grease the threads so that they go in easily.

Cut the two internal cockpit stiffeners which are each 1 ft $5\frac{1}{2}$ in × 2 in × $\frac{3}{4}$ in.

Cut off the bottom outside corners of the cockpit ends to form 1 × 1 in triangular limber (drain) holes which will be next to the sides and bottom of the hull (see plan 2.7).

7·Cutting out the parts for the centre-line (bow stiffener) backbone and dagger-board casing

Cut out the centre-line backbone (shown shaded on plan 2.3) from the 8 in × $\frac{3}{4}$ in planking to match the bottom curve of the forward 2 ft 9 in of the side pieces. This is slightly too long but modifications come later at the aft and forward ends. Cut off the forward $2\frac{3}{8}$ in so that the fore end will meet the stem when assembled (plan 2.6). Cut the aft end at the same angle as WZ, 19 degrees to the vertical (see plan 2.3).

For the dagger-board casing cut out two side pieces (see plan 2.3). Then cut out item VWZ. Cut out an identical shape (to VWZ) from plywood. (This may be obtained from surplus pieces cut out of the deck for the cockpit well, etc. See below.) Cut out a further piece of ply to go in the overlap between the centre-line backbone and the casing.

When gluing up the casing (see below) remember the ply inserts at each end which are fitted on the starboard side only (see plan 2.4) to make the casing slot a little wider than the dagger-board. Secure either end of the dagger-board casing with two screws (at each end). Cut a 1 × 1 in V-notch to form a limber (drain) hole on the lower edge of the centre-line backbone just forward of the dagger-board casing.

8·First gluing session

(a) Glue the two stem pieces together (take out the screws, glue the surfaces to be joined, then screw back together).

(b) Glue up the cockpit sides and ends (take out screws, glue the surfaces to be joined, then screw back together).

(c) Glue up the backbone and dagger-board casing (take out screws, glue the surfaces to be joined, then screw back together).

(d) Glue up the tiller (take out screws, glue the surfaces to be joined, then screw back together).

(e) Glue up the dagger-board.

Wipe off surplus glue.

9·Deck – marking out on the underside

Take one of the 8 ft × 4 ft sheets of ply and lay it down on a *flat* floor.

(a) Mark the centre-line down the 8 ft length.

(b) At the bow put marks 1 ft $5\frac{1}{4}$ in either side of the centre-line and a second mark $\frac{3}{4}$ in inside these to show where both sides of the side pieces come.

(c) Follow the same procedure as at (b) at the stern: marks at 1 ft $9\frac{3}{4}$ in and 1 ft 9 in from the centre-line (ie either side of the side pieces).

(d) Mark out the cockpit well. The aft end of the well is 2 ft 6 in from the aft end of the deck.

(e) Put the cockpit well/bulkhead unit in place and draw all round inside, *but do not cut to this line.* Make sure the cockpit well sides are parallel to each other and to the centre-line.

(f) Mark a line 4 in inside each cockpit well side. This shows where the deck opening for the cockpit comes. At the corners make a radius (curved corner) of 1 in.

(g) Mark the access hatch with the centre 6 in aft of the after side of the cockpit well.

(h) Lay down the centre-line backbone piece and dagger-board casing forward of the cockpit well and make sure it is exactly on the centre-line. Draw all round outside. Remove the centre-line backbone piece and dagger-board casing, determine the exact position of the dagger-board slot and then mark this.

Now cut out the dagger-board slot $1\frac{1}{4}$ in wide, cut out the hatchway and lastly cut out the cockpit well.

10·Making the spars

Cut the 2 in × 2 in timber pieces to the lengths required for the rig you have chosen and as shown on the plan for the mast, gaff and boom (2.1). Taper both ends of the gaff and boom and one end of the mast as follows:

(a) Draw a line around the spar 2 ft 6 in from the end.

(b) Mark the extreme end of the spar $\frac{1}{2}$ in in from each edge on each side.

(c) Join the marks at the extreme ends and the mark at 2 ft 6 in from the end.

(d) Cut away all four taper pieces at each end (you will have to renew your marks as successive pieces are cut away) and then plane the spars smooth removing all sharp edges to achieve a slightly rounded finish, except at the untapered base of the mast which should remain square.

At the bottom of the mast cut a recess $\frac{1}{2}$ in deep and $\frac{3}{4}$ in up the mast to fit the mast step on the deck (see plan 2.8).

Drill $\frac{5}{16}$ in holes horizontally each end of the boom and gaff, and countersink (see plan 2.9).

Add the following chocks to the boom: (i) on top at the outer end for the end of the sheet, (ii) on one side 2 ft 6 in from the end for a sheet block, (iii) on one side 5 ft 5 in from the end for a sheet block and (iv) on the port side 7 ft 11 in from the end for the mast tie. In addition, fit two chocks to the mast-head (see plan 2.9).

TOP RIGHT Plan 2.8 Mast step dimensions and cockpit bottom stiffeners.

BOTTOM RIGHT Plan 2.9 Boom, gaff and mast details.

For dimensions of the chocks see plan 2.9. Chocks are better practice than too many holes, since they do not weaken the spar.

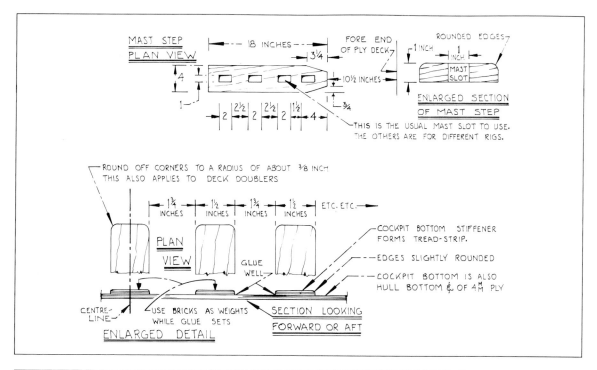

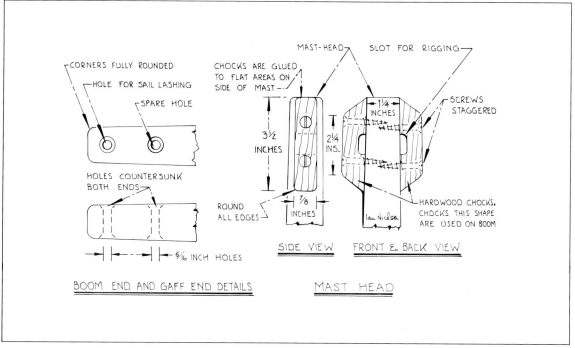

11·Assembling parts on the underside of the deck

(a) Mark the middle of the transom on the inside. Stand it on edge on the deck which is laid down on a flat floor.

(b) Mark the middle of the stem piece and lay it at the forward end of the deck which it overlaps by $1\frac{3}{4}$ in.

(c) Lay down the cockpit well/bulkhead unit in the correct place over its hole. Lay the cockpit deck stiffeners in position (see plan 2.6) and secure with one screw at each end through the cockpit ends.

Plan 2.10 Method of holding sides in place at bow during fitting and gluing.

(d) Lay down the boat's sides and put two screws into the upper edge of each side piece at approximately $4\frac{1}{2}$ in and $6\frac{1}{2}$ in from the forward end.

(e) Put thin rope round the sides and transom at the stern and round the four screws at bow (see plan 2.10).

(f) Pull in the sides at the stern then the bow, by winding rope 'Spanish windlass' style (see plan 2.10), to the double marks (see 9(b) and (c)) on the ply deck which show where the side pieces come.

(g) Put two screws through each side into (i) the forward and aft ends of the cockpit well, (ii) the sides of the transom, (iii) the stem pieces at the bow.

(h) Put centre-line backbone and dagger-board casing in place.

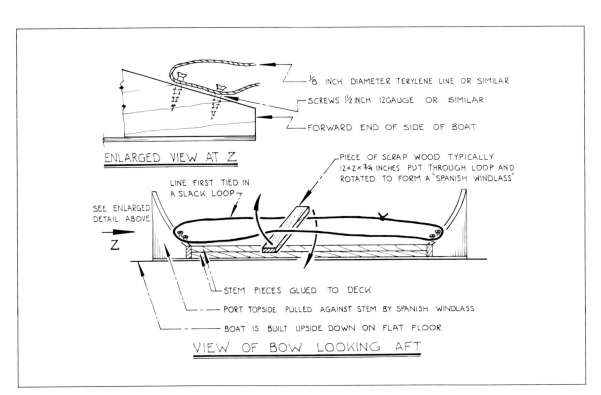

ENLARGED VIEW AT Z

$\frac{1}{8}$ INCH DIAMETER TERYLENE LINE OR SIMILAR

SCREWS $1\frac{1}{2}$ INCH 12 GAUGE OR SIMILAR

FORWARD END OF SIDE OF BOAT

PIECE OF SCRAP WOOD TYPICALLY 12×2×¾ INCHES PUT THROUGH LOOP AND ROTATED TO FORM A "SPANISH WINDLASS"

LINE FIRST TIED IN A SLACK LOOP

SEE ENLARGED DETAIL ABOVE

Z

STEM PIECES GLUED TO DECK

PORT TOPSIDE PULLED AGAINST STEM BY SPANISH WINDLASS

BOAT IS BUILT UPSIDE DOWN ON FLAT FLOOR

VIEW OF BOW LOOKING AFT

12·Joining of sides, cockpit well/bulkhead unit, transom and stem piece – second gluing session

Take the whole assembly off the deck and put it on paper or polythene sheet on a flat floor.

Release the screws at the transom and slack off the aft Spanish windlass. Release the screws (at aft end of cockpit) which go through the sides, apply glue here and rescrew. Put glue on the ends of the transom. Put the screws back here, using the Spanish windlass to pull the sides into the transom.

Now do the same at the bow. Release the stem piece side screws and slack off the Spanish windlass. Release the side screws at the fore end of the cockpit, put glue in here, replace screws. Put glue on at the stem ends. Put screws back, using the Spanish windlass to pull the sides together again. Let the glue harden.

When the glue has set put the framework on the underside of the deck and pencil all round inside and out, then lift the whole framework and stand it on one side piece. Plane the edges of the framework, if necessary, so that it will lie flush on the deck.

13·Joining of the complete frame to the underside of the deck – third gluing session

Apply glue all round to the frame edge, spread well and lay the frame down on the deck at the pencil marks. Place the backbone/dagger-board casing assembly on the deck and also the locker sides. Screw and glue. The locker ends have one screw at each joint and two screws should be used through the fore end of the cockpit to secure the aft end of the dagger-board casing. Remember to glue all joins including the join with the underside of the deck.

Let the glue harden and then carefully cut off surplus ply at the edge of the deck (the surplus may be used later for deck stiffeners) and plane flush with the sides.

Paint the underside of the deck and interior framework with metallic primer at this stage, also one side (the inside) of the remaining ply sheet which is to form the bottom of the hull.

IMPORTANT **Do not apply primer to surfaces which are to be glued subsequently, ie lower edges of the framework and corresponding areas on the ply bottom.**

14·Fitting and gluing on ply bottom

Lay the deck and framework down on a *flat* surface. Take the ply sheet which is to form the bottom and select which end is to be the stern. Then, by careful measurement from the stern of the framework, establish the exact position of the dagger-board slot and mark it on the ply bottom and cut it out. Lay the ply bottom over the framework, carefully lining up the rear of the ply sheet with the transom. Remove the ply bottom and plane any 'high spots' on the frame so that the ply bottom will lie flush. Screw the bottom down to the transom with at least four well spread 1 in 8-gauge screws. Then, by applying even pressure, ensure the bottom is lying flush with the stern half of the underside of the boat and put in two screws amidships either side to secure the ply. Then 'smooth' the ply down over the forward section to the bow and put at least four well-spaced screws into the stem and bow ends of the side pieces. Then put screws at even spacing (approximately 6 in–8 in) all round through the ply into the sides, stem and transom, and also round the dagger-board slot.

Now remove the screws and lift off the ply bottom. Apply glue evenly to the lower edges of the framework, replace the ply bottom and rescrew.

Allow the glue to harden, then carefully cut off surplus ply at the edges of the bottom and plane flush with the sides. (Again remember the surplus may be used later for deck stiffeners.)

15·Bottom rubbers and deck fittings

Now cut the bottom rubbers (rubbing strakes) (using 8 ft 6 in × 1 in × $\frac{3}{8}$ in pieces for the long pair and offcuts from the planks for the short pair at the sides) to the lengths shown on plan 2.2. Bevel the ends. Secure to the

Plan 2.11 Break-water.

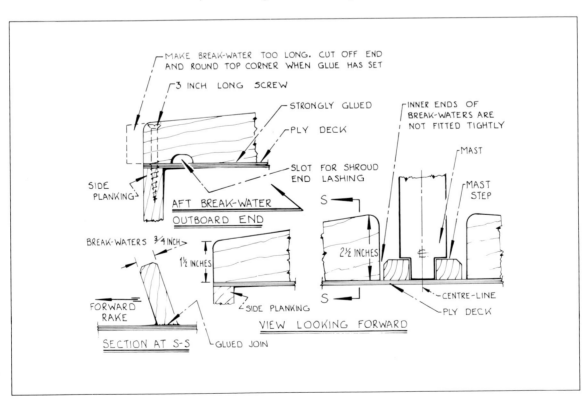

bottom (where shown on plan 2.7) with glue along the entire length and screws at either end.

Now turn the complete hull the right way up. Cut the break-waters (2.11), transom capping piece (both parts, 2.7) and mast step (2.8) to the sizes shown on the plans, using the remaining sections of $\frac{3}{4}$ in planking. Plane and finish these pieces (break-waters should be tapered and bevelled and include a slot each side on the underside, as shown on plan 2.11, for shroud attachment) and place them all on the deck *exactly* where indicated on plan 2.2. Pencil round the outlines. Cut the ply cockpit bottom stiffeners and deck doublers to the required dimensions, and plane and sandpaper them smooth. Place them in appropriate positions as indicated on plan 2.2 and pencil round the outlines. Now glue both parts of the transom capping piece together and allow the glue to harden. Then glue all the deck and cockpit fittings in place using large screws to secure outer ends of the breakwaters through the deck into the side pieces. Also put two screws through the rear part of the transom capping piece and deck into the transom.

Allow the glue to harden, then ensure all edges of the hull are finished properly and *fill any cracks or openings between the sides, deck and bottom and inside the cockpit with glue, slightly thickened.*

16·Painting

Paint the hull and deck with at least one coat of marine primer, two coats of marine undercoat and one coat of yacht enamel, allowing adequate drying time and preparing the surface with sandpaper before each coat.

Paint the inside of the dagger-board slot by wrapping cloth round a thin piece of wood, dipping it in paint, then poking it into the slot and applying paint to the sides of the casing.

You may wish to varnish the deck in which case a minimum of four coats will be required, the first being of slightly thinned varnish. Again allow adequate drying time and sandpaper between each coat.

The spars, dagger-board, rudder and tiller should be varnished as above.

17·Rigging your Cove Boat

Two small plastic cleats must be screwed to the mast 8 in–10 in above the base: one is situated on the aft side, the other on the starboard side. The halyard block should be tied to the masthead on the port side and the halyard led through and down to the aft cleat. The other cleat is used in due course to secure the mast-to-boom tie which is taken through the chock on the boom, round the mast and secured to the cleat.

Now tie the shrouds and forestay to the mast-head (use 6 mm super pre-stretched three-strand rope for the stays). Place the mast in the mast-step, hold the mast raked aft and secure the shrouds to the breakwaters ensuring that the mast is not tilted to port or starboard. Apply tension to the shrouds by tightening the forestay through the bow handhold. This is best done by tying a loop near the base of the forestay and passing some 4 mm rope through this loop and the bow handhold several times.

Ask your local sailmaker (or one advertising cruising and/or dinghy sails in the yachting press) to make up a sail for you to the dimensions shown on the plan. Show the sail plan (2.1) to the sailmaker so that he can get a good idea of the rig used on this boat. The sail is attached to the gaff by a lashing at either end, through the holes and around the gaff at the eyes in the sail. The halyard may also be attached round the gaff and through one of the sail eyes.

Photo 2.2 *Cove boat* and her spars and equipment are easily transported.

The foot of the sail should be tied securely to both ends of the boom through the holes on the boom. The boom should be tied closely at its forward end to the base of the gaff.

Now hoist your sail on the port side of the mast. It may need tensioning and setting. Do this by adjusting or tightening the lashings round and at the ends of the spars and tightening down on the mast-to-boom tie described above. Rig the mainsheet as shown on the plan using blocks tied to the transom and the chocks on the boom.

You may wish to fly a burgee. This is best tied to the end of the gaff.

Please remember always to wear a life-jacket.

CHAPTER 3
Longa 11 feet 10 inches overall

Longa is a very simple, very stable, fully-decked sailing dinghy for one or two people. *Longa* won the 1984 Royal Yachting Association 'Design and build a sailing dinghy for under £200' competition at the UK National Dinghy Exhibition in London. The concept of this boat is based on the use of four 8 ft × 4ft sheets of marine plywood. *Longa* is suitable for construction by someone without previous boatbuilding experience

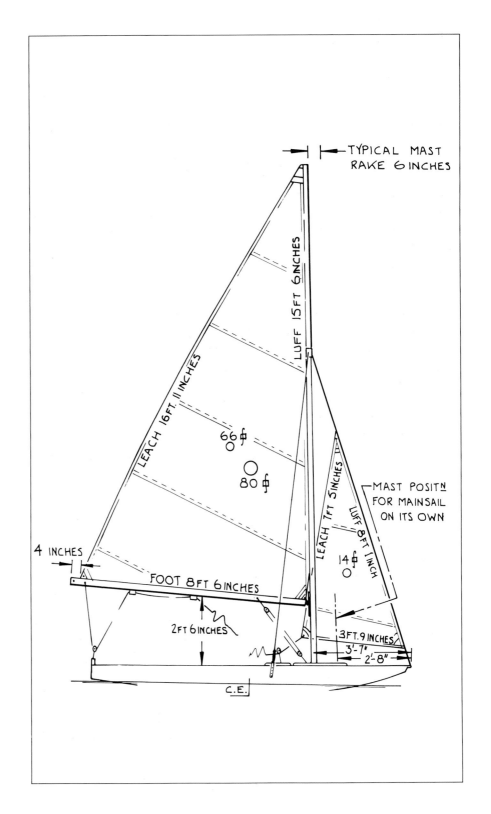

Plan 3.1 Low Sail plan.

who has knowledge of basic woodworking skills. No special tools are required. *Longa*, for all her simplicity, looks surprisingly elegant on the water and she rewards the owner with a quite sparkling performance.

Before we had even finished *Cove Boat*, it began to dawn on us that there was excellent potential for an enlarged semi-sistership. The name *Longa* can be seen as a play on words as it is the name of a small island off the north-west coast of Scotland.

What we did not bargain for was that the Royal Yachting Association would decide to run a competition to 'design and build a sailing dinghy for under £200', with the final judging of entries to take place at the UK National Dinghy Exhibition in London in March 1984, the year after we built *Cove Boat*! The design of *Longa* was complete when the competition was announced, late in 1983. The concept of *Longa* was ideally suited to the competition and we could not resist the challenge. The boat had to be tried and tested before the judging took place and photographs were required to prove it. A January launch date was unavoidable. Ian's diary for 21 January 1984 reads: 'Gareloch – Wind: Force 6 and rising. Sea state: rough and getting worse. Land conditions: deep snow drifting.' We could not get a dinghy trailer down to the beach because of deep snow, and at one stage we slid the boat over the snow like a sledge.

Sail we did in that howling, frigid wind. Apart from some initial trouble keeping the rudder down (which was later solved) *Longa* behaved impeccably. However, it is not normally advisable to carry out the first day's trials of a boat in strong conditions and we urge our readers to do as we say (see Chapter 8 on safety), and not do as we did on that day!

▶ LONGA – WOOD REQUIREMENTS

1. Four sheets 8 ft × 4 ft marine ply 4 or 5 mm ($\frac{3}{16}$ in) thick. We would suggest at least two of the sheets should be varnishing grade for the deck. *Longa* looks particularly attractive with a varnished deck.
2. Main stem piece: 1 ft 10 in × 4 in × $\frac{3}{4}$ in white pine.
3. Bow transom: 2 ft × 3$\frac{1}{2}$ in × $\frac{3}{4}$ in white pine.
4. Doubler for handgrip slot: 8 in × 1$\frac{1}{4}$ in × $\frac{3}{4}$ in hardwood.
5. Keelson: 4 ft 4 in × 3$\frac{1}{2}$ in × $\frac{3}{4}$ in white pine.
6. Centreline underdeck stiffener: 4 ft 2 in × 2 in × $\frac{3}{4}$ in white pine.
7. Pillars under foredeck: two pieces made from 1 ft 2 in × 1$\frac{1}{2}$ in × $\frac{3}{4}$ in white pine.
8. Three foredeck beams: total length 9 ft 6 in × 1$\frac{1}{2}$ in × $\frac{3}{4}$ in white pine.
9. Stiffeners under foredeck fore-end: two pieces 1 ft 8 in × 1$\frac{1}{2}$ in × $\frac{3}{4}$ in white pine.
10. Foredeck aft stiffeners: four pieces 2 ft 1 in each × 1$\frac{1}{2}$ in × $\frac{3}{4}$ in white pine.
11. Three transverse bottom stiffeners: total length 9 ft 6 in × 1$\frac{1}{2}$ in × $\frac{3}{4}$ in white pine.
12. Two breakwaters: one piece 2 ft 6 in × 5 in × $\frac{3}{4}$ in cut diagonally into two pieces 2 ft 6 in × 3$\frac{1}{2}$ in at inner end and 1$\frac{1}{2}$ in at outer end. Hardwood.
13. Mast step: one piece (ideally hardwood) 2 ft × 6 in × 1 in.
14. Bottom rubbers: two pieces 10 ft 6 in

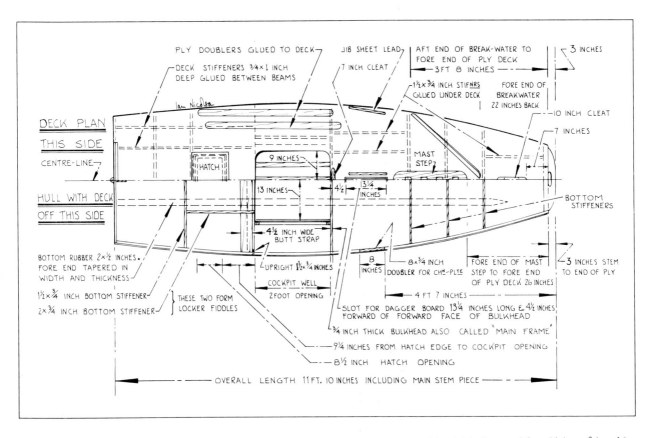

Plan 3.2 Hull and deck plan.

14. × 2 in × $\frac{1}{2}$ in white pine. Two pieces 2 ft 6 in × $\frac{3}{4}$ in × $\frac{3}{4}$ in white pine.

15. Chain-plate doublers: two pieces 9 in × 8 in × $\frac{3}{4}$ in white pine.

16. Jib sheet leads: four pieces 12 in × $\frac{3}{4}$ in × $\frac{3}{4}$ in hardwood.

17. Cleats: assorted lengths hardwood up to 10 in × $1\frac{1}{2}$ in × 1 in.

18. Dagger-board: lengths of $\frac{3}{4}$ in thick white pine free from knots to make up an area 3 ft long × 1 ft wide, eg three pieces 3 ft × 4 in × $\frac{3}{4}$ in.

19. Top strips on dagger-board: total length 1 ft 6 in × $\frac{3}{4}$ in × $\frac{3}{4}$ in preferably hardwood.

20. Fore-end of dagger-board case: 1 ft 1 in × 5 in × $\frac{3}{4}$ in white pine.

21. Aft end of dagger-board case: 1 ft × 4 in × $\frac{3}{4}$ in white pine.

22. Dagger-board case sides: two pieces 1 ft 8 in × 11 in × $\frac{3}{4}$ in white pine. (To get 11 in width, edge-gluing may be required).

23. Main frame: 4 ft × 11 in × $\frac{3}{4}$ in white pine.

24. Upper and lower cockpit side stiffeners: four pieces total length 8 ft 6 in × $1\frac{1}{2}$ in × $\frac{3}{4}$ in white pine.

25. Cockpit side vertical stiffeners: four pieces 8 in × $1\frac{1}{2}$ in × $\frac{3}{4}$ in white pine.

26. Cockpit fillet pieces: two pieces 2 ft × $\frac{3}{4}$ in × $\frac{3}{4}$ in white pine.

27. Aft end of cockpit stiffeners top and bottom: two pieces 4 ft × $1\frac{1}{2}$ in × $\frac{3}{4}$ in white pine. Additional vertical stiffeners: two pieces 8 in × $1\frac{1}{2}$ in × $\frac{3}{4}$ in white pine.

28. Cockpit edge stiffeners: two pieces 2 ft × $1\frac{1}{2}$ in × $\frac{3}{4}$ in white pine.

29. Deck edge stringers: two pieces 12 ft 4 in × $1\frac{1}{2}$ in × $\frac{3}{4}$ in white pine.

30. Bottom stringers: two pieces 12 ft 4 in × $1\frac{1}{2}$ in × $\frac{3}{4}$ in white pine.

31. Aft deck beams: two pieces 3 ft 9 in × $1\frac{1}{2}$ in × $\frac{3}{4}$ in white pine.

32. Aft deck stringers: four pieces made

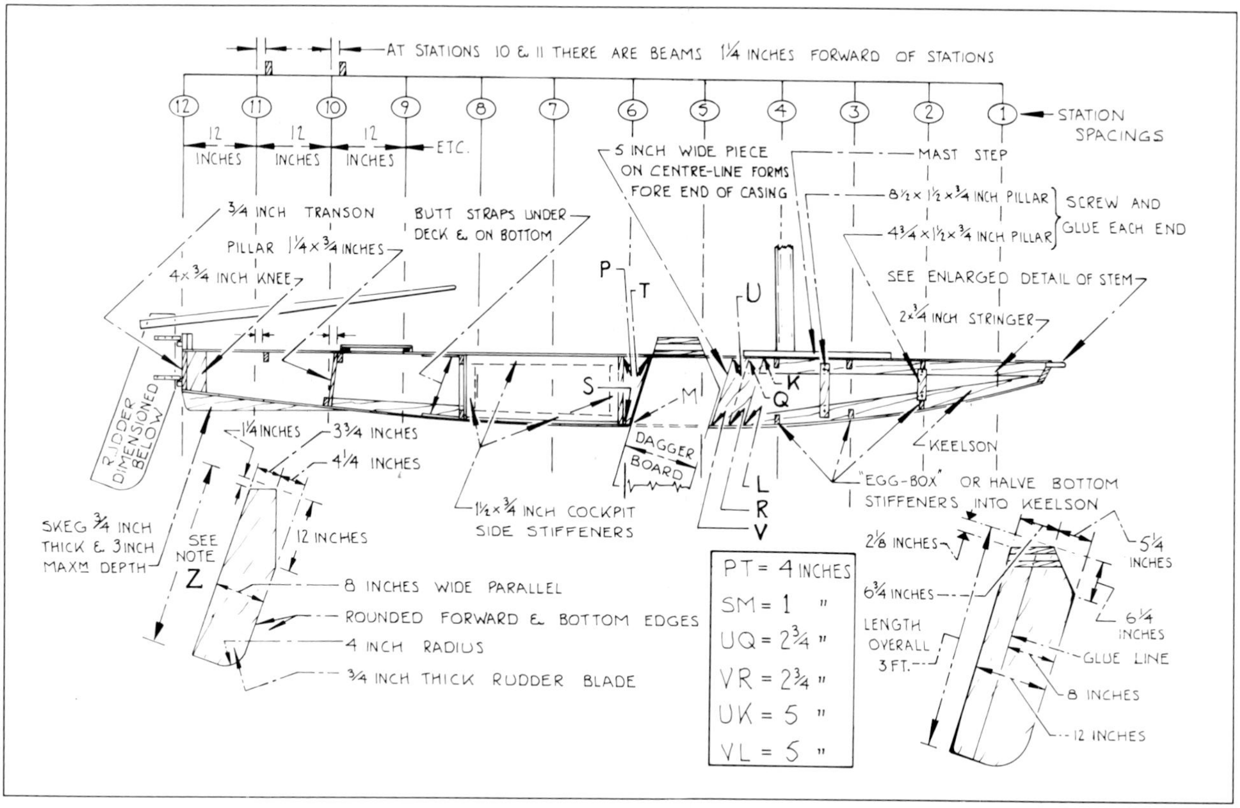

AT STATIONS 10 & 11 THERE ARE BEAMS 1¼ INCHES FORWARD OF STATIONS
12
11
10
9
8
7
6
5
4
3
2
1
STATION SPACINGS
12 INCHES
12 INCHES
12 INCHES
ETC.
5 INCH WIDE PIECE ON CENTRE-LINE FORMS FORE END OF CASING
MAST STEP
8½ × 1½ × ¾ INCH PILLAR
4¾ × 1½ × ¾ INCH PILLAR
SCREW AND GLUE EACH END
¾ INCH TRANSON
PILLAR 1¼ × ¾ INCHES
4 × ¾ INCH KNEE
BUTT STRAPS UNDER DECK & ON BOTTOM
P
T
U
SEE ENLARGED DETAIL OF STEM
2 × ¾ INCH STRINGER
S
M
K
Q
RUDDER DIMENSIONED BELOW
1¼ INCHES
3¾ INCHES
4¼ INCHES
DAGGER BOARD
KEELSON
"EGG-BOX" OR HALVE BOTTOM STIFFENERS INTO KEELSON
L
R
V
1½ × ¾ INCH COCKPIT SIDE STIFFENERS
SKEG ¾ INCH THICK & 3 INCH MAXM DEPTH
SEE NOTE
Z
12 INCHES
8 INCHES WIDE PARALLEL
ROUNDED FORWARD & BOTTOM EDGES
4 INCH RADIUS
¾ INCH THICK RUDDER BLADE
PT = 4 INCHES
SM = 1 "
UQ = 2¾ "
VR = 2¾ "
UK = 5 "
VL = 5 "
2⅛ INCHES
5¼ INCHES
6¾ INCHES
6¼ INCHES
LENGTH OVERALL 3 FT.
GLUE LINE
8 INCHES
12 INCHES

up from 15 ft 6 in × 1 in × $\frac{3}{4}$ in white pine.

33. Aft bottom athwartships stiffener: one piece 3 ft 9 in × $1\frac{1}{2}$ in × $\frac{3}{4}$ in white pine.
34. Bottom stiffeners forming locker fiddles: two pieces 1 ft 11 in × 2 in × $\frac{3}{4}$ in white pine.
35. Aft deck pillar: one piece 9 in × $1\frac{1}{4}$ in × $\frac{3}{4}$ in white pine.
36. Transom: one piece 3 ft 4 in × 6 in × $\frac{3}{4}$ in white pine.
37. Transom knee: one piece 7 in × 4 in × $\frac{3}{4}$ in white pine.
38. Transom top piece: two pieces 2 ft × $2\frac{3}{4}$ in × $\frac{3}{4}$ in white pine.
39. Hatch coamings: two pieces 10 in × $\frac{3}{4}$ in × $\frac{3}{4}$ in white pine; two pieces 1 ft 4 in × $\frac{3}{4}$ in × $\frac{3}{4}$ in white pine.
40. Hatch lid edging pieces: two pieces 1 ft × $\frac{3}{4}$ in × $\frac{3}{4}$ in white pine; two pieces 1 ft 6 in × $\frac{3}{4}$ in × $\frac{3}{4}$ in white pine.
41. Hatch lid sealing pieces: two pieces 1 ft 1 in × 1 in × $\frac{3}{8}$ in white pine; two pieces 1 ft 7 in × 1 in × $\frac{3}{8}$ in white pine.
42. Skeg: one piece 2 ft 3 in × 3 in × $\frac{3}{4}$ in white pine.
43. Rudder: one piece 2 ft 5 in × 8 in × $\frac{3}{4}$ in hardwood.
44. Rudder box: two pieces 1 ft × 8 in × $\frac{3}{4}$ in hardwood. Filler pieces and stringers: total length 2 ft 9 in × 1 in × $\frac{3}{4}$ in hardwood.
45. Tiller: one piece 4 ft 4 in × $1\frac{3}{4}$ in × $\frac{3}{4}$ in hardwood. (Should be cut to length after trials.)

Plan 3.3 Hull section. NOTE z The total length of the rudder is normally 2 ft 5 in, but it may be made 2 ft 9 in if extra windward ability is required.

▶ LONGA – CONSOLIDATED WOOD LIST

NO. OF
PIECES

Marine plywood 8 ft × 4 ft sheets
4 4 or 5 mm ($\frac{3}{16}$ in) varnishing or
   painting grade

White pine $1\frac{1}{2}$ in × $\frac{3}{4}$ in
4 12 ft 4 in
2 9 ft 6 in **11, 8**
1 8 ft 6 in **24**
2 4 ft
3 3 ft 9 in
4 2 ft 1 in
2 2 ft
2 1 ft 8 in
1 1 ft 2 in **7**
6 8 in

White pine $\frac{1}{2}$ in
2 10 ft 6 in × 2 in

White pine $\frac{3}{8}$ in
2 1 ft 7 in × 1 in
2 1 ft 1 in × 1 in

White pine $\frac{3}{4}$ in
1 4 ft × 11 in
2 1 ft 8 in × 11 in
2 9 in × 8 in
1 3 ft 4 in × 6 in
1 1 ft 1 in × 5 in
3 3 ft × 4 in **18**
1 1 ft 10 in × 4 in

1 1 ft × 4 in
1 7 in × 4 in
1 4 ft 4 in × $3\frac{1}{2}$ in
1 2 ft × $3\frac{1}{2}$ in
1 2 ft 3 in × 3 in
2 2 ft × $2\frac{3}{4}$ in
1 4 ft 2 in × 2 in
2 1 ft 11 in × 2 in
1 9 in × $1\frac{1}{4}$ in
1 15 ft 6 in × 1 in **32**
2 2 ft 6 in × $\frac{3}{4}$ in
2 2 ft × $\frac{3}{4}$ in
2 1 ft 6 in × $\frac{3}{4}$ in
2 1 ft 4 in × $\frac{3}{4}$ in
2 1 ft × $\frac{3}{4}$ in
2 10 in × $\frac{3}{4}$ in

Hardwood
1 2 ft × 6 in × 1 in
1 10 in × $1\frac{1}{2}$ in × 1 in **17**
1 2 ft 5 in × 8 in × $\frac{3}{4}$ in
2 1 ft × 8 in × $\frac{3}{4}$ in
1 2 ft 6 in × 5 in × $\frac{3}{4}$ in
1 4 ft 4 in × $1\frac{3}{4}$ in × $\frac{3}{4}$ in
1 8 in × $1\frac{1}{4}$ in × $\frac{3}{4}$ in
1 2 ft 9 in × 1 in × $\frac{3}{4}$ in **44**
1 1 ft 6 in × $\frac{3}{4}$ in × $\frac{3}{4}$ in **19**
4 1 ft × $\frac{3}{4}$ in × $\frac{3}{4}$ in

Numbers in bold type refer to items in 'Wood requirements'.

▶ LONGA – BUILDING NOTES

Please read these notes right through before commencing construction. You will be able to save time and material by carrying out gluing or varnishing of certain components in batches.

All screws used should be made of brass, bronze or stainless steel. We used two-part epoxy glue produced by Structural Polymer Systems Ltd. A metric conversion table is on page 101.

The concept of this boat is based on the use of four 8 ft × 4 ft sheets of marine plywood 4 or 5 mm thick. Make sure that the plywood sheets are fully 8 ft × 4 ft, and not slightly under these dimensions.

Making the deck

This boat is built upside down. The building sequence commences, therefore, with laying out the deck. Cut one of the sheets of plywood exactly in half to give two 4 ft × 4 ft pieces. At the newly cut edges of these pieces, cut off strips 4½ in wide (and 4 ft long). Take a further sheet of uncut ply, plus one of the 3 ft 7½ in × 4 ft pieces, and lay them down on

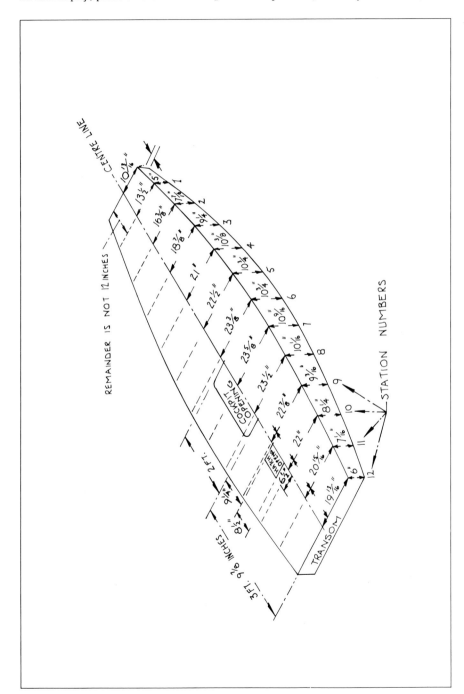

Plan 3.4 Hull dimensions with offsets. IMPORTANT The vertical dimensions do not include the thickness of the deck or bottom ply. Therefore the sides should be made to the dimensions shown. The stations are at 12 in intervals, starting from the aft face of the transom. The angle between the sides and the deck and bottom is 90 degrees throughout the boat's length.

a flat floor to make a rectangle 8 ft plus 3 ft $7\frac{1}{2}$ in long, ie 11 ft $7\frac{1}{2}$ in × 4 ft. Now mark the longitudinal centre-line. Starting from the stern (where the 3 ft $7\frac{1}{2}$ in piece is) intervals of 12 in are marked off. Mark offsets, as shown on the isometric plan (3.4), from one side of the centre-line. Join up the offset marks using a stiff wooden batten. Get two or three people to help hold the batten, or use heavy weights to hold it down. Cut off the surplus deck material very carefully and use the offcut pieces as templates to mark out the other side, then cut out this as well.

Place the two parts of the deck on the flat floor once again. One of the $4\frac{1}{2}$ in × 4 ft pieces which have already been cut is used as a 'butt strap' to join the two pieces of deck. Mark the location of the butt strap on the two pieces of ply to be joined. The butt strap overlaps the aft piece of ply by $2\frac{1}{4}$ in and the forward piece by $2\frac{1}{4}$ in. Now trim the butt strap so that its outer edges are 1 in inside the outer deck line. This is to allow space for deck stringers and ply topsides to be fitted later. Now glue the butt strap precisely in place over the deck join.

Making the transom

Cut out the transom from solid pine. Its dimensions are 3 ft 4 in (minus 2 × 4 mm for ply topsides) × 6 in × $\frac{3}{4}$ in. Bevel each side to suit the angle between the transom and the topsides. Bevel the bottom of the transom to suit the angle of the bottom of the hull, which is approximately 6 degrees. In practice this involves planing $\frac{1}{16}$ in off the aft edge of the bottom of the transom. At this stage the lower rudder pintle should be bolted on.

Making the main frame

The main frame is located with its aft face 5 ft $9\frac{7}{8}$ in forward of the aft face of the transom. Its dimensions are 3 ft 11 in, minus 2 × 4 mm for the ply sides (check this at the boat), × $10\frac{3}{4}$ in × $\frac{3}{4}$ in. Make sure the main frame is exactly rectangular. Because the main frame is $10\frac{3}{4}$ in deep, it may be necessary, depending upon available timber, to edge-glue two pieces together. At all four corners make $1\frac{1}{2}$ in × $\frac{3}{4}$ in cut-outs for the deck and bottom stringers to be fitted later (see plan 3.5). At the cut-outs for the bottom stringers, additional small triangular pieces approximately 1 in × 1 in should be cut away for limber (drain) holes.

The main frame and the transom can now be glued in position on the underside of the deck. An additional internal knee is used (see dimensions shown on plan 3.3) to support the transom.

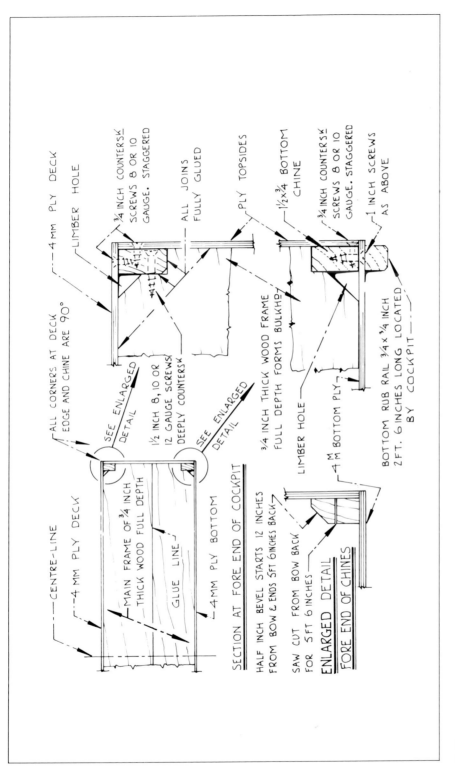

4MM PLY DECK

LIMBER HOLE

¾ INCH COUNTERSK SCREWS 8 OR 10 GAUGE. STAGGERED

ALL JOINS FULLY GLUED

PLY TOPSIDES

½×¾ BOTTOM CHINE

¾ INCH COUNTERSK SCREWS 8 OR 10 GAUGE. STAGGERED

1 INCH SCREWS AS ABOVE

ALL CORNERS AT DECK EDGE AND CHINE ARE 90°

SEE ENLARGED DETAIL

SEE ENLARGED DETAIL

¾ INCH THICK WOOD FRAME FULL DEPTH FORMS BULKHD

LIMBER HOLE

4 M BOTTOM PLY

BOTTOM RUB RAIL ¾×¾ INCH 2FT. 6 INCHES LONG LOCATED BY COCKPIT

CENTRE-LINE

4 MM PLY DECK

MAIN FRAME OF ¾ INCH THICK WOOD FULL DEPTH

GLUE LINE

4MM PLY BOTTOM

1½ INCH 8, 10 OR 12 GAUGE SCREWS DEEPLY COUNTERSK

SECTION AT FORE END OF COCKPIT

HALF INCH BEVEL STARTS 12 INCHES FROM BOW & ENDS 5FT 6INCHES BACK

SAW CUT FROM BOW BACK FOR 5FT 6 INCHES

ENLARGED DETAIL
FORE END OF CHINES

Plan 3.5 Main frame and chines.

29

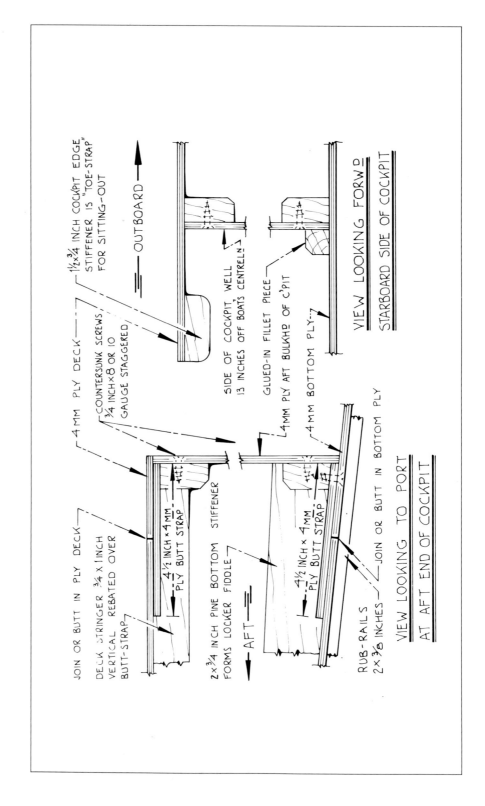

1½×¾ INCH COCKPIT EDGE
STIFFENER IS "TOE-STRAP"
FOR SITTING-OUT

← OUTBOARD

4MM PLY DECK

COUNTERSUNK SCREWS
¾ INCH×8 OR 10
GAUGE STAGGERED

SIDE OF COCKPIT WELL
13 INCHES OFF BOATS CENTRELN

GLUED-IN FILLET PIECE

4MM PLY AFT BULKHD OF C'PIT

4MM BOTTOM PLY

VIEW LOOKING FORW'D
STARBOARD SIDE OF COCKPIT

JOIN OR BUTT IN PLY DECK

DECK STRINGER ¾×1 INCH
VERTICAL REBATED OVER
BUTT-STRAP

← AFT

4½ INCH×4MM
PLY BUTT STRAP

2×¾ INCH PINE BOTTOM STIFFENER
FORMS LOCKER FIDDLE

4½ INCH×4MM
PLY BUTT STRAP

RUB-RAILS
2×⅜ INCHES

JOIN OR BUTT IN BOTTOM PLY

VIEW LOOKING TO PORT
AT AFT END OF COCKPIT

Plan 3.6 Cockpit details.

30

Making the cockpit

Ensure that there is sufficient ply of suitable dimensions set aside for the topsides (see below), and also a whole and a half sheet remaining for the bottom. The aft end of the cockpit and the cockpit sides can be marked out and cut from the remaining ply. The dimensions of the aft end of the cockpit are 29 in × 10 in. Solid pine athwartships stiffeners $1\frac{1}{2}$ in × $\frac{3}{4}$ in are screwed and glued close to the top and bottom of the ply, leaving 4 mm clear above the upper stiffener and 4 mm clear below the lower stiffener for the thickness of the butt straps (see plan 3.6). These stiffeners are the full width of the boat, less an allowance as before for the dimensions of the stringers and limber holes. Additional upright pieces of solid pine $1\frac{1}{2}$ in × $\frac{3}{4}$ in are fitted either side between the outer ends of the top and bottom stiffeners (see plan 3.2), remembering to allow for the top and bottom stringers and the limber holes. The cockpit sides can now be cut out. They are 24 in long, $10\frac{3}{4}$ in deep at the forward end and 10 in deep at the aft end. However it is best to start by cutting out a rectangle 24 in × $10\frac{3}{4}$ in to which are glued $1\frac{1}{2}$ in × $\frac{3}{4}$ in pine stiffeners on all four edges. The cockpit sides are now marked port- and starboard-handed. The bottom of the sides can be planed later to suit the curvature of the bottom of the boat. The cockpit can now be screwed and glued together and to the underside of the deck in the position shown on plan 3.2.

Deck beams

Make deck beams out of $1\frac{1}{2}$ in × $\frac{3}{4}$ in pine to appropriate lengths, remembering to allow for the thickness of the sides at each end as before (ie 1 in to allow for stringer plus ply topside). These are required at stations 2, 3, 4, 10 and 11. Note that the deck beams at stations 2, 3 and 4 go on the aft side of the station line, while 10 and 11 go $1\frac{1}{4}$ in forward of the station line. The deck beam ends are bevelled to suit the deck edge line. The deck beams can now be glued in position on the underside of the deck.

Aft deck stringers

Aft deck stringers $\frac{3}{4}$ in × 1 in deep are now cut to length and glued to the underside of the deck between the transom, the beam by station 11, the beam by station 10 and the cockpit (see plans 3.2 and 3.3).

Making the dagger-board casing

For the dagger-board casing cut out two sides of solid wood, not ply (see PQRS on plan 3.3). Cut out item PTMS in one thickness ($\frac{3}{4}$ in) of solid wood. Cut out an identical shape PTMS in ply (using an off-cut). Cut out in solid wood ($\frac{3}{4}$ in thick) item UKLV and a piece of ply UQRV (using an offcut).

When gluing up remember the ply filler pieces at each end, located on the starboard side only, to make the casing 4 mm (about $\frac{1}{8}$ in) wider than the dagger-board thickness. Secure both ends of the casing with at least three screws almost right through.

Having constructed the dagger-board casing, plane off the top so that it will fit perfectly when laid upside down on the under side of the deck. The aft edge of the casing is planed smooth so that it will abut perfectly onto the forward face of the main frame.

Now mark on the underside of the deck the hole for the dagger-board slot in the following way. Carefully lift and support the structure above the floor, then mark out the slot for the dagger-board by marking two parallel lines, each line $\frac{5}{8}$ in either side of the centre-line, from the forward side of the main frame to the third deck beam (which is on station 4). Lay the dagger-board casing on its side on the deck with the

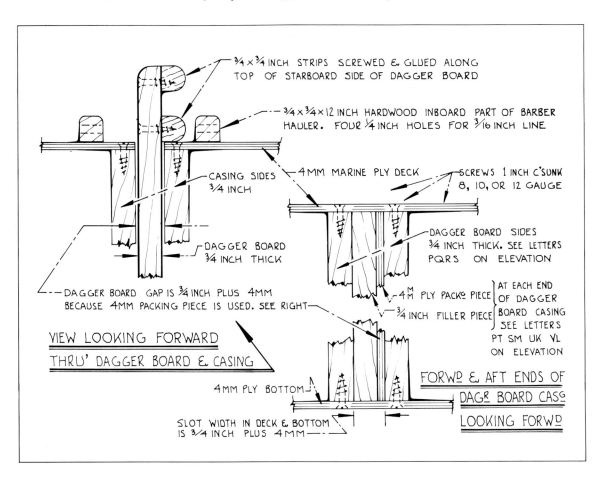

¾ × ¾ INCH STRIPS SCREWED & GLUED ALONG TOP OF STARBOARD SIDE OF DAGGER BOARD

¾ × ¾ × 12 INCH HARDWOOD INBOARD PART OF BARBER HAULER. FOUR ¼ INCH HOLES FOR ³⁄₁₆ INCH LINE

CASING SIDES ¾ INCH

4MM MARINE PLY DECK

SCREWS 1 INCH C'SUNK 8, 10, OR 12 GAUGE

DAGGER BOARD SIDES ¾ INCH THICK. SEE LETTERS PQRS ON ELEVATION

DAGGER BOARD ¾ INCH THICK

DAGGER BOARD GAP IS ¾ INCH PLUS 4MM BECAUSE 4MM PACKING PIECE IS USED. SEE RIGHT

VIEW LOOKING FORWARD THRU' DAGGER BOARD & CASING

4M PLY PACK⁵ PIECE
¾ INCH FILLER PIECE

AT EACH END OF DAGGER BOARD CASING SEE LETTERS PT SM UK VL ON ELEVATION

4MM PLY BOTTOM

SLOT WIDTH IN DECK & BOTTOM IS ¾ INCH PLUS 4MM

FORW⁰ & AFT ENDS OF DAG⁵ BOARD CAS⁵ LOOKING FORW⁰

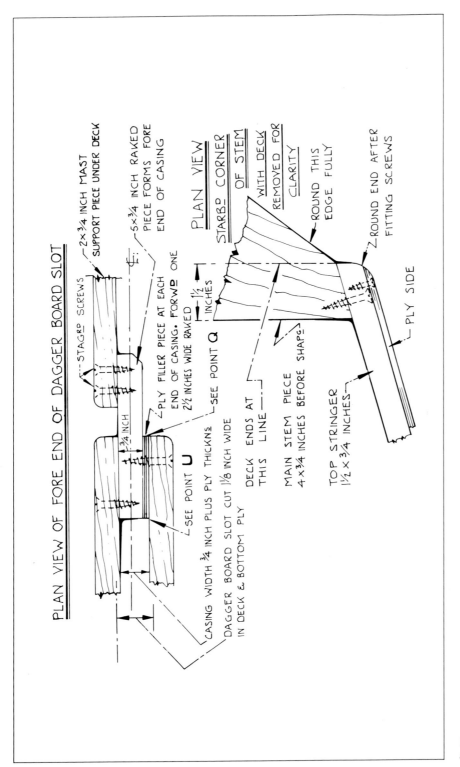

PLAN VIEW OF FORE END OF DAGGER BOARD SLOT

2 × ¾ INCH MAST
SUPPORT PIECE UNDER DECK

5 × ¾ INCH RAKED
PIECE FORMS FORE
END OF CASING

STAGRD SCREWS

PLAN VIEW
OF STEM
STARB'D CORNER

WITH DECK
REMOVED FOR
CLARITY

PLY FILLER PIECE AT EACH
END OF CASING. FORW'D ONE
2½ INCHES WIDE RAKED

SEE POINT Q

ROUND THIS
EDGE FULLY

1½
INCHES

ROUND END AFTER
FITTING SCREWS

¾ INCH

SEE POINT U

PLY SIDE

DECK ENDS AT
THIS LINE

CASING WIDTH ¾ INCH PLUS PLY THICKN'S

MAIN STEM PIECE
4 × ¾ INCHES BEFORE SHAPG

DAGGER BOARD SLOT CUT 1⅛ INCH WIDE
IN DECK & BOTTOM PLY

TOP STRINGER
1½ × ¾ INCHES

Plan 3.8 Dagger-board slot
and stem detail.

33

top of the case parallel to the centre-line and $\frac{5}{8}$ in away. Mark a line $\frac{1}{4}$ in forward of the fore end of the slot and another $\frac{1}{4}$ in aft of the aft end of the slot. Cut out at these lines and down the lines $\frac{5}{8}$ in off the centre-line described above. This gives a slot in the ply deck larger than the slot in the dagger-board case so that the ply edges are not chipped when the dagger-board is raised and lowered. Due to the 4 mm ply packing piece in the case, the case is not centered exactly on the centre-line of the boat. The dagger-board casing can now be glued in position, ensuring ample glue is applied at the join with the underside of the deck and the join with the main frame. Two screws should be inserted from the aft face of the main frame into the end of the case to hold it precisely and firmly.

Photo 3.2 Deck upside-down on a flat floor. Main frame, cockpit sides, deck beams and dagger-board casing have been fitted.

Centre-line underdeck stiffener

Cut out this piece from solid pine with dimensions 4 ft 2 in (approximately) $\times$ 2 in $\times$ $\frac{3}{4}$ in. The fore end of this piece slopes to support the bow transom and it slots over each cross-deck stiffener/beam so that its top edge is glued to the underside of the deck. Make sure there is ample glue where each slot fits over a deck beam. The aft end of the piece is screwed to the side of the 5 in $\times$ $\frac{3}{4}$ in centre forward piece of the dagger-board case. If a bolt $1\frac{3}{4}$ in long is available, use it here instead of two screws. The forward end of the centre-line underdeck stiffener is slightly angled in to lie on the centre-line of the boat.

Making the stem and bow transom

Make up the main stem piece from solid pine 2 ft $\times$ 4 in $\times$ $\frac{3}{4}$ in. Clamp the deck stringers (for dimensions see below) in their place at the forward

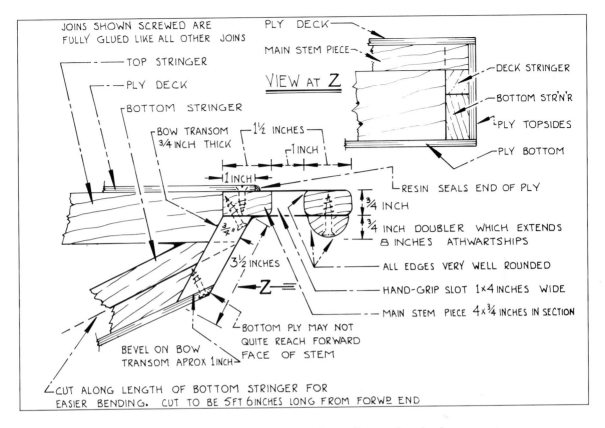

end of the deck and fit the stem piece between them flat on the deck.

Cut out the bow transom from a piece of solid pine slightly wider than the aft end of the main stem piece (see plan 3.9 and check measurement at the boat). Again the bow transom should be $\frac{3}{4}$ in thick and it is $3\frac{1}{2}$ in top to bottom. Bevel the top edge of the bow transom by planing away the aft side of this edge to a depth of $\frac{7}{16}$ in. Then bevel the bottom edge of the bow transom by planing away the forward side of this edge to a depth of 1 in. (See section detail on plan 3.9). The stem piece and bow transom can now be glued together and subsequently glued in position.

Plan 3.9 Stem and bow transom.

Making the deck edge stringers

Cut these from $1\frac{1}{2}$ in × $\frac{3}{4}$ in solid pine. The aft end must butt onto the transom forward face, lie against the ends of all deck beams and overlap the edges of the main stem piece. Provisionally fit the deck stringers in position using clamps and rope to pull the ends in at the bow. The stringers can be screwed in position through the stern transom and screwed on the ends of all deck beams and the bow transom. Remove the stringers, glue all joins and screw back together. Ensure that the join between the upper edge of the stringer and underside of the deck is well glued and held tight at all points while the glue sets. The forward ends of the stringers can be trimmed flush with the bow transom later.

The holes for the cockpit and the hatch may now be marked on the underside of the deck and cut out. The cockpit hole dimensions are 24 in fore and aft and 18 in athwartships with rounded corners as shown on plan 3.2. The hole for the hatch should be $8\frac{1}{2}$ in fore and aft and 14 in athwartships, the fore edge of this hole being $9\frac{1}{4}$ in aft of the aft edge of the cockpit.

Two holes should be drilled through the transom near the bottom and well outboard to take two bungs which can now be fitted.

Making the keelson

To make the keelson, which runs from the bottom forward corner of the dagger-board case to the stem, cut it from pine 4 ft 4 in (approximately) $\times 3\frac{1}{2}$ in $\times \frac{3}{4}$ in.

Its top edge is straight and its bottom edge follows the same curve as the sides, so until the sides are finally fitted and glued in position its bottom shape is not finalised. This is done by laying a level batten across the sides and cutting off the 'high points' from the keelson. Leave it $\frac{1}{16}$ in high over the aft 2 ft 3 in of its bottom edge to put a very slight bow in the bottom of the boat. The keelson can now be screwed and glued in position.

Fit pillars between keelson and centre-line underdeck stiffener. The forward pillar is $4\frac{3}{4}$ in $\times 1\frac{1}{2}$ in $\times \frac{3}{4}$ in and is tight up under the forward deck beam; the aft pillar is $8\frac{1}{2}$ in $\times 1\frac{1}{2}$ in $\times \frac{3}{4}$ in and is fitted 9 in forward of the dagger-board case (see plan 3.3). Glue and fix each end of each pillar with one bolt or two screws.

Making the sides

The ply sides are each made from two pieces of ply joined with the use of a $4\frac{1}{2}$ in butt strap. In the sides the join is situated forward, at approximately station 4. Mark out the aft and forward ends of one side on a piece of ply by setting verticals off a straight base line every foot, then mark offsets starting with the transom. Use a batten to obtain a fair line. Cut out the two pieces for one side and then use them as templates for marking and cutting out the other side. The ply sides must fit tight against the top and bottom stringers throughout their length, therefore the butt straps cannot lap the whole join. A $1\frac{1}{2}$ in space at either end of the join must be left clear to allow flush fitting of the sides. Now mark the precise position of each butt strap having in mind these criteria. The sides must be port- and starboard-handed with the butt straps on the inside of each join. The two pieces of each side can now be glued together with the use of heavy weights (bricks or similar) placed over the butt straps.

When the glue has set the sides can be put in place. Make sure the sides are a good fit. Secure with a screw at the transom (stern) and then put a screw every 16 in or so into the deck stringer, then drill extra screw holes between the former ones so that the sides can be secured all along with screws at 8 in centres. Now remove the sides. Prepare to glue on one of the sides (it is recommended that each side should be put on at a separate gluing session) by making sure that the deck is lying completely flat and fully supported at all points. If you cannot find a floor that is flat enough try supporting the entire deck and framework on top of two or more stout and straight planks laid on edge. Glue the side to the deck stringer, transom and stem using screws at the pre-drilled holes 8 in apart to hold the side while the glue sets.

Bottom stringers

To make the bottom stringers, cut off two pieces of pine 12 ft 4 in × $1\frac{1}{2}$ in × $\frac{3}{4}$ in with as few knots as possible; the forward half must have no knots at all. Plane all faces, then plane the bevel along the top inboard edges, except the forward 1 ft (see plan 3.9). Make a cut in the knot-free end 5 ft 6 in long, from the forward end along the middle of the $1\frac{1}{2}$ in face.

Photo 3.3 Bottom stringer clamped in position while glue sets. Note that the keelson has also been fitted.

The bottom stringers can now be fitted one at a time in separate gluing sessions. Proceed by firstly screwing (with $1\frac{1}{2}$ in 8-gauge screws) the stringer at the stern. Put a screw through the transom into the end of the stringer so that it will be held close next to the ply side. Then (again using $1\frac{1}{2}$ in 8-gauge screws) put screws through the ply sides and stringer into firstly the *ends* of the aft cockpit framework and then the ends of the main frame. Now bend the forward end of the stringer, which is longitudinally sliced 5 ft 6 in back for easier bending (see above), and secure to the bow transom with $1\frac{1}{2}$ in screws while ensuring both halves of the split stringer are clamped together. Secure the ply to the stringer between the main fixing points using small screws well countersunk. Remove all screws and apply glue to the appropriate surfaces of the stringer (including inside the 5 ft 6 in cut). Put the stringer in position and, starting from the stern, resecure with screws and clamps to hold in position while the glue sets. Repeat the process for the stringer on the other side.

A number of transverse stiffeners are fitted between the bottom stringers at stations 2, 3, 4 and on the aft side of station 10. These are made from $1\frac{1}{2}$ in $\times$ $\frac{3}{4}$ in solid pine and are cut to appropriate lengths so that they will abut to the bottom stringers. The forward stiffeners and the lower edge of the keelson must be notched where they cross them. At the outer lower edges of all the stiffeners small triangular pieces should be cut away to make limber holes. They can now be screwed and glued in position and their lower edges should be slightly bevelled to correspond to the curvature of the bottom of the boat. A vertical pillar should be added amidships between the deck and bottom stiffeners at station 10 for extra strength (see plan 3.3).

It is important to ensure at this stage that the lower edges of the cockpit framework, dagger-board case and keelson follow the curvature of the bottom of the boat. This is done by using a straight batten laid across the bottom and planing away any wood which stands high, but remembering to leave the keelson $\frac{1}{16}$ in high over the aft 2 ft 3 in of its bottom edge, all as described earlier under 'Making the keelson'.

Additional stiffening of the sides is required internally in way of the chain-plates. In order to allow flexibility in the choice of rig, these stiffeners, which are made from $\frac{3}{4}$ in thick solid pine, should extend from 4 ft 7 in to 5 ft 3 in aft of the extreme forward end of the stem. The stiffeners should also extend the full depth of the sides between the top and bottom stringers.

Making and fitting the bottom

Lay an 8 ft $\times$ 4 ft sheet of ply on the bottom with the centre-line of the ply at the forward end on the centre-line of the bow transom. The centre-line of the ply at the aft end should be on the centre-line of the boat found by measuring in from both sides. Hold the ply down with weights and pencil round outboard of the topsides. Now get under the boat and with a pencil tightly tied to a piece of 16 in × $\frac{1}{2}$ in × $\frac{1}{2}$ in wood mark up through the dagger-board slot onto the ply. Mark round inside the bottom of the cockpit and also establish the available overlap internally for the transverse butt strap (this should be 2 in to $2\frac{1}{4}$ in). Note that the butt strap slides between the bottom ply and the cockpit aft stiffener. Remove the ply from the hull and cut out the slot for the dagger-board, making the slot too short and narrow so that it can be cut to exact size when the ply has finally been glued down. Paint or varnish this piece of ply keeping clear of areas round edges, cockpit, centre-line, bottom stiffeners and butt strap (see below) which will subsequently be glued. Paint or varnish the inside of the hull.

Photo 3.4 Bottom is fitted. The forward ply sheet has been screwed and glued in position and the butt strap is glued in position ready to accept the smaller aft piece of the ply bottom.

The large bottom sheet can now be screwed in position with screws into the bottom stringers, the bow transom and the bottom of the dagger-board casing, all at approximately 8 in centres. Now remove the ply, apply glue to the edges of the bow transom, sides, keelson, bottom stiffeners, dagger-board case, main frame and cockpit, then screw the ply back in position. The ply should be weighted down in way of the bottom stiffeners, main frame and cockpit while the glue sets to ensure a tight join. Bricks or bags of dry sand may be used for this.

The remaining $4\frac{1}{2}$ in × 4 ft piece (see under 'Making the deck') is now used to make the butt strap. It is $4\frac{1}{2}$ in fore and aft and the full width athwartships, less 1 in either end in way of the sides. The butt strap can then be glued in position internally athwartships and wedged while the glue sets. Because the butt strap slides between the ply and the cockpit aft stiffener, this should help hold it in position. The forward edge of the butt strap which overlaps the cockpit aft stiffener should also be glued. When the glue has set the smaller aft piece of ply bottom can be marked up, cut to size, painted internally (except over areas to be glued) and screwed and glued in position. When the glue has set, bottom rubbers and skeg cut to dimensions shown on the plan can be glued in place on the bottom with the use of weights.

When the glue has hardened the boat can be turned over.

The cockpit floor is stiffened internally by gluing the rectangular piece, cut out of the deck earlier, to the floor. Additional fore-and-aft ply doublers are glued on top of this to provide extra stiffness and a better grip for the feet when sailing. Cockpit edge stiffeners cut from solid pine $1\frac{1}{2}$ in × $\frac{3}{4}$ in are glued port and starboard under the inboard edge of the

Plan 3.10 Aft locker hatch and break-water.

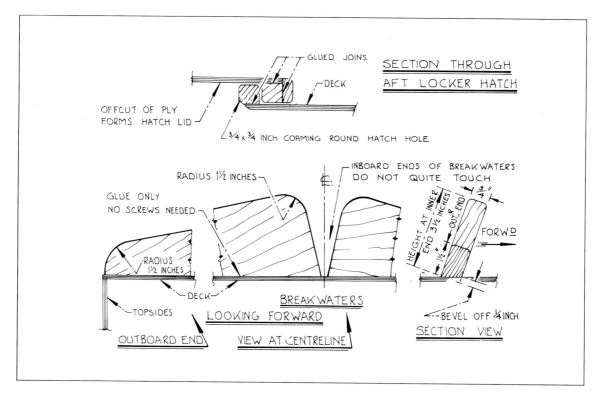

deck. These act as 'toe straps' for sitting out and their ends as well as their top faces must be well glued. Solid pine fillet pieces 24 in × $\frac{3}{4}$ in × $\frac{3}{4}$ in are made up and glued in position where the cockpit sides meet the bottom. Additional fillet gluing should now be carried out internally all round where the sides and ends meet the ply bottom to make a really strong watertight join. Aft of the cockpit inside the hatch additional fore-and-aft bottom stiffeners are glued to the bottom as shown on plan 3.2.

Make up break-waters (plan 3.10), mast step (also see below under

Plan 3.11 Bow and stern details.

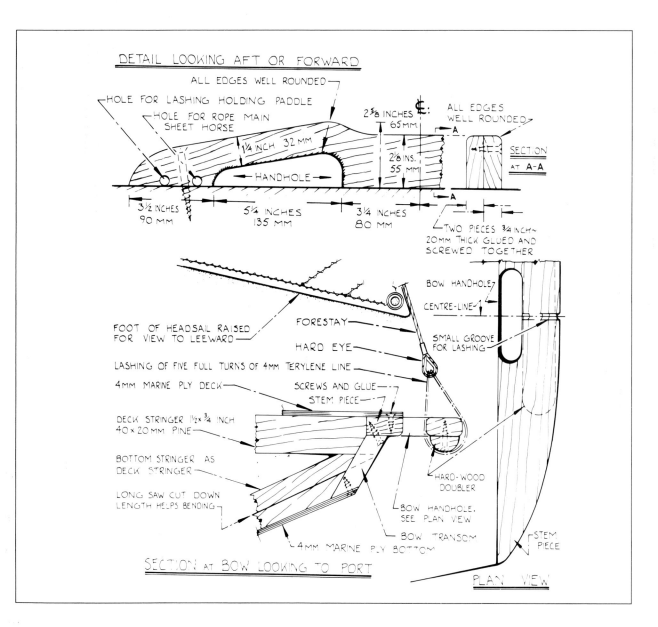

41

'Rig') and transom top piece which is made from two identical pieces of $\frac{3}{4}$ in thick solid pine (plan 3.11). See the plan for the shapes of these parts. Remember when bevelling the break-waters to make them port- and starboard-handed. The wooden coaming pieces for the aft hatch (3.10) the two cleats (3.12) and the four ply deck doublers (3.2) should also be made up to dimensions shown on the plans. All these deck fittings can now be glued (and screwed where appropriate) in position. Use bricks or similar weights to hold the parts while the glue sets.

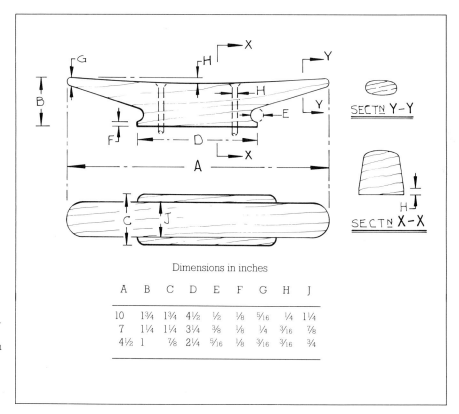

Dimensions in inches

A	B	C	D	E	F	G	H	J
10	1¾	1¾	4½	½	⅛	⁵⁄₁₆	¼	1¼
7	1¼	1¼	3¼	⅜	⅛	¼	³⁄₁₆	⅞
4½	1	⅞	2¼	⁵⁄₁₆	⅛	³⁄₁₆	³⁄₁₆	¾

Plan 3.12 Cleat dimensions. A cleat is known by its overall length (column A in the table). Cleats should be made of hardwood and given four coats of yacht varnish.

The dagger-board (3.3), rudder and rudder box if required (3.13), tiller and hatch lid should be made up to the dimensions shown on the plans. The rudder should have a rounded forward edge and tapered aft edge. The rudder fittings can then be attached and the upper pintle bolted to the transom upper piece.

Rig

Buy a suitable second-hand rig of between 75 and 90 sq. ft and cut slots of the mast step to suit. Screw on the chain-plates at the correct location and sloped forward to line up with the shrouds; then remove them again to simplify painting of the hull (use chain-plates with at least three securing holes). The screw holes will remain visible to show where they are refitted when painting is complete.

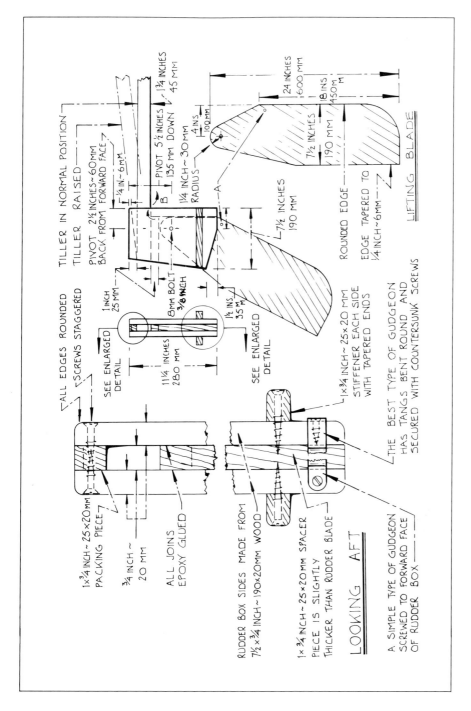

Plan 3.13 Rudder dimensions and details.

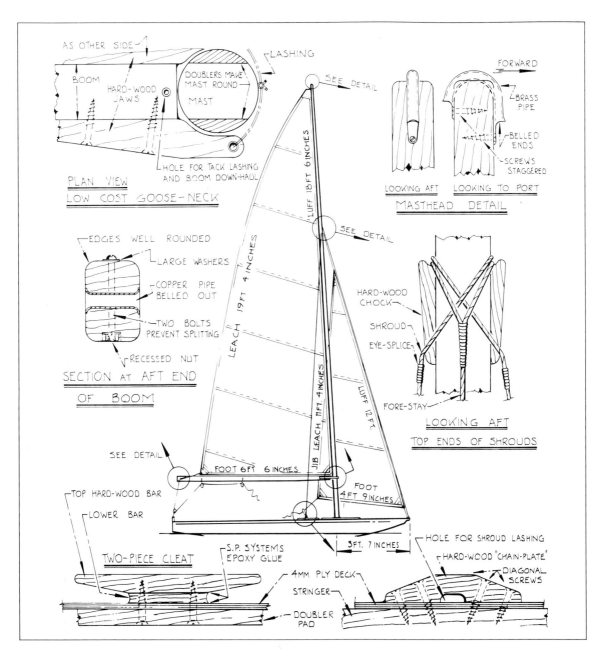

Plan 3.14 High sail plan and rigging details.

Painting

The entire hull and fittings should now be painted and/or varnished according to the owner's choice. When painting, it is important to use good-quality marine primer, undercoat and enamel. If varnishing, use at least four coats of marine varnish, the first coat being thinned to manufacturer's recommendations.

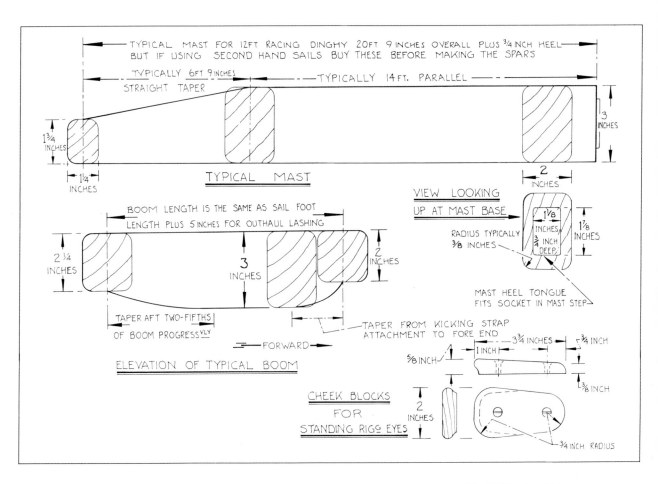

TYPICAL MAST FOR 12FT RACING DINGHY 20FT 9 INCHES OVERALL PLUS ¾ INCH HEEL
BUT IF USING SECOND HAND SAILS BUY THESE BEFORE MAKING THE SPARS

TYPICALLY 6FT 9 INCHES
STRAIGHT TAPER

TYPICALLY 14 FT. PARALLEL

1¾ INCHES

3 INCHES

1¼ INCHES

2 INCHES

TYPICAL MAST

VIEW LOOKING
UP AT MAST BASE

1⅛ INCHES

1⅛ INCHES

¾ INCH DEEP

RADIUS TYPICALLY ⅜ INCHES

MAST HEEL TONGUE
FITS SOCKET IN MAST STEP

BOOM LENGTH IS THE SAME AS SAIL FOOT
LENGTH PLUS 5 INCHES FOR OUTHAUL LASHING

2¼ INCHES

3 INCHES

2 INCHES

TAPER AFT TWO-FIFTHS
OF BOOM PROGRESSᵛˡʸ

TAPER FROM KICKING STRAP
ATTACHMENT TO FORE END

FORWARD

ELEVATION OF TYPICAL BOOM

3¾ INCHES

¾ INCH

5⅛ INCH

1 INCH

1⅜ INCH

CHEEK BLOCKS
FOR
STANDING RIGG EYES

2 INCHES

¾ INCH RADIUS

Plan 3.15 Mast and boom
dimensions and rigging
detail.

45

CHAPTER 4
Kilda 11 feet 6 inches overall

Kilda is a performance sailing dinghy for an agile crew of two under all conditions and one person under light conditions. She has a relatively sophisticated hull shape and consequently requires more advanced construction techniques than other boats in this book. Many of the techniques are much simpler, however, than in other boats of her type and no specialist tools are required. Experience of building another dinghy, such as *Longa*, is recommended before tackling this project.

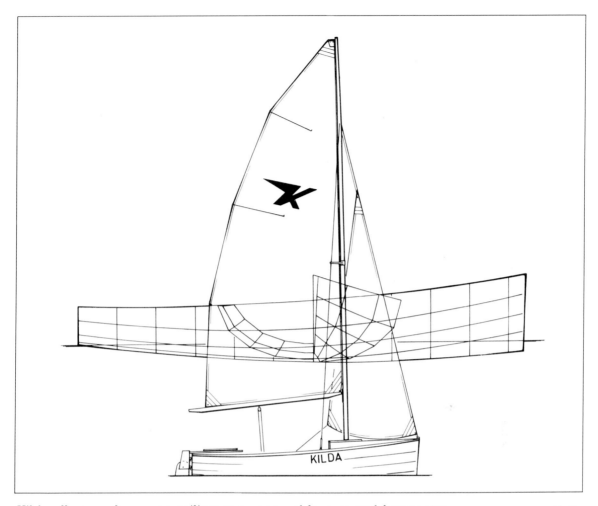

Plan 4.1 Sail plan and hull lines.

Kilda offers performance sailing at a reasonable cost and her pretty appearance attracts admirers everywhere.

We were at the UK National Dinghy Exhibition in London, pleased with ourselves having just won the 'Design and Build a Sailing Dinghy for under £200' competition with *Longa*. We were in no sense dissatisfied with *Longa*, but, having the boatbuilding bug in a bad way, the question on both our minds was 'What next?' We took a good look at some of the beautifully finished, but costly craft on show and thought 'Wouldn't it be fun to produce a performance dinghy with a sophisticated hull shape and the looks to match.'

The problem is that sophistication often means complications and high cost. The bywords for producing our previous dinghies had been low cost and simplicity. The aim with the new boat would be a shapely planing hull that the amateur with a little experience could build cheaply.

Wood was the natural choice of material. By using two-part epoxy glue we were able to eliminate many of those complicated bevels which can be so troublesome and time-consuming when building a boat of this type. With simple home-made wooden clamps it is possible to build a lapstrake hull having only four planks a side without expensive tools.

Kilda is a superb boat to sail, being fast and responsive. Because of her shape and the tall 90 sq ft rig she demands more agility from her crew than does *Longa* or *Cove Boat*. However, there is a rich reward in the sheer thrill of sailing fast!

▶ KILDA – WOOD REQUIREMENTS

1. Three 8 ft × 4 ft sheets 6 mm ($\frac{1}{4}$ in) varnishing or painting grade marine plywood for planks, butt straps and dagger-board case sides.

2. Stem: one piece 3 ft × 5 in × $\frac{3}{4}$ in hardwood.
   Stem laminations: two pieces 2 ft 1 in × 5 in × $\frac{3}{4}$ in softwood; one piece 1 ft 8 in × 3 in × $\frac{3}{4}$ in softwood.
   Stem capping piece: 6 in × 3 in × $\frac{3}{4}$ in hardwood.
   Stem knee: $5\frac{1}{2}$ in × $3\frac{1}{4}$ in × $\frac{5}{8}$ in hardwood.

3. Hog: one piece 11 ft 6 in × 5 in × $\frac{1}{2}$ in hardwood.
   Additional lamination: 2 ft 6 in × width to suit (approximately 4 in) × $\frac{1}{2}$ in hardwood.

4. Keelson: one piece 5 ft × $2\frac{1}{4}$ in × $\frac{5}{8}$ in hardwood; one piece 4 ft 3 in × 3 in × $\frac{5}{8}$ in hardwood.

5. Frames (not deck beams): up to 28 ft total length × 5 in × $\frac{5}{8}$ in hardwood may be required, but savings should be possible with careful arrangement of frame patterns.
   Transom top: 4 ft 2 in × $2\frac{3}{4}$ in × $\frac{5}{8}$ in hardwood.
   Transom pillar: 8 in × $3\frac{3}{4}$ in × $\frac{5}{8}$ in hardwood.

6. Foredeck beam station 2: one piece 1 ft 10 in × 3 in × $\frac{3}{4}$ in hardwood.
   Foredeck beam station 5: one piece 4 ft 1 in × 6 in × $\frac{7}{8}$ in hardwood.

7. Thwart support beam at frame by station 7: one piece 4 ft × $2\frac{1}{4}$ in × $\frac{3}{4}$ in hardwood.

   Thwart support beam at frame by station 10: one piece 4 ft × $2\frac{1}{4}$ in × $\frac{1}{2}$ in hardwood.
   Thwart at frame by station 7: one piece 4 ft 1 in × $2\frac{3}{4}$ in × $\frac{3}{4}$ in hardwood.
   Thwart at frame by station 10: one piece 4 ft × $2\frac{3}{4}$ in × $\frac{3}{4}$ in hardwood.

8. Chain-plate pads: two pieces 9 in × 7 in × $\frac{3}{8}$ in hardwood.

9. Mast pillars: two pieces 1 ft 8 in × $1\frac{3}{4}$ in × $\frac{7}{8}$ in hardwood.
   Doublers for mast pillars: four pieces 2 ft × 3 in × $\frac{3}{4}$ in softwood.
   Mast step: one piece 1 ft 8 in × 3 in × 1 in hardwood.

10. Foredeck stringers: one piece 4 ft 5 in × $2\frac{1}{2}$ in × $\frac{3}{4}$ in softwood; four pieces 3 ft 2 in × 2 in × $\frac{1}{2}$ in softwood.

11. Gunwhale rubbing strakes: four pieces 13 ft × $1\frac{1}{2}$ in × $\frac{5}{8}$ in softwood; two pieces 8 ft 4 in × $1\frac{1}{2}$ in × $\frac{5}{8}$ in softwood.
    Gunwhale rubbing strake capping pieces: two pieces 7 ft × 4 in × $\frac{1}{4}$ in hardwood; two pieces 5 ft × 4 in × $\frac{1}{4}$ in hardwood.

12. Quarter knees: two pieces 11 in × $2\frac{3}{8}$ in × $\frac{3}{4}$ in hardwood.

13. Transom centre-line doubler: one piece 14 in × $3\frac{3}{4}$ in × $\frac{3}{4}$ in hardwood.

14. Aft thwart support knee: one piece $7\frac{1}{2}$ in × 6 in × $\frac{5}{8}$ in hardwood.

15. Break-waters: two pieces 2 ft 2 in × 4 in × $\frac{1}{4}$ in hardwood.

16. Dagger-board case stiffeners: top two pieces 2 ft × $1\frac{1}{2}$ in × $\frac{7}{8}$ in hardwood; lower two pieces 2 ft × $3\frac{3}{4}$ in × $\frac{7}{8}$ in hardwood.

Dagger-board case filler pieces: one piece 1 ft 9 in × 2 in × $1\frac{1}{8}$ in hardwood; one piece 1 ft 3 in × 2 in × $1\frac{1}{8}$ in hardwood.

17. Dagger-board: two pieces 4 ft × 9 in × $\frac{7}{8}$ in yellow pine or hardwood.

18. Mainsheet traveller support: one piece 2 ft 2 in × $3\frac{1}{2}$ in × 1 in hardwood.

19. Rudder: one piece 2 ft 6 in × $7\frac{1}{2}$ in × $\frac{3}{4}$ in yellow pine or hardwood.

20. Rudder box: two pieces 12 in × 8 in × $\frac{3}{4}$ in hardwood.
Filler pieces and stringers: total length 2 ft 9 in × 1 in × $\frac{3}{4}$ in hardwood.

21. Tiller: one piece 3 ft × $1\frac{1}{4}$ in × $\frac{3}{4}$ in hardwood.
Tiller extension: one piece 3 ft × 1 in × $\frac{5}{8}$ in hardwood.

▶ KILDA – CONSOLIDATED WOOD LIST

NO. OF
PIECES

Marine plywood 8 ft × 4 ft sheets
3   6 mm ($\frac{1}{4}$ in) varnishing or painting grade

Hardwood $1\frac{1}{8}$ in
1   1 ft 9 in × 2 in
1   1 ft 3 in × 2 in

Hardwood $\frac{3}{4}$ in
2   1 ft × 8 in
1   3 ft × 5 in
1   1 ft 2 in × $3\frac{3}{4}$ in
1   1 ft 10 in × 3 in
1   6 in × 3 in
1   4 ft 1 in × $2\frac{3}{4}$ in
1   4 ft × $2\frac{3}{4}$ in
2   11 in × $2\frac{3}{8}$ in
1   4 ft × $2\frac{1}{4}$ in
1   3 ft × $1\frac{3}{4}$ in
1   2 ft 9 in × 1 in

Hardwood $\frac{3}{8}$ in
2   9 in × 7 in

Hardwood 1 in
1   2 ft 2 in × $3\frac{1}{2}$ in
1   1 ft 8 in × 3 in

Hardwood $\frac{5}{8}$ in
1    $7\frac{1}{2}$ in × 6 in
1   28 ft × 5 in
1   8 in × $3\frac{3}{4}$ in
1    $5\frac{1}{2}$ in × $3\frac{1}{4}$ in
1   4 ft 3 in × 3 in
1   4 ft 2 in × $2\frac{3}{4}$ in

1   5 ft × $2\frac{1}{4}$ in
1   3 ft × 1 in

Hardwood $\frac{1}{4}$ in
2   7 ft × 4 in
2   5 ft × 4 in
2   2 ft 2 in × 4 in

Hardwood $\frac{7}{8}$ in
1   4 ft 1 in × 6 in
2   2 ft × $3\frac{3}{4}$ in
2   1 ft 8 in × $1\frac{3}{4}$ in
2   2 ft × $1\frac{1}{2}$ in

Hardwood $\frac{1}{2}$ in
1   11 ft 6 in × 5 in
1   2 ft 6 in × 4 in
1   4 ft × $2\frac{1}{4}$ in

Yellow pine/hardwood
2   4 ft × 9 in × $\frac{7}{8}$ in
1   2 ft 6 in × $7\frac{1}{2}$ in × $\frac{3}{4}$ in

Softwood $\frac{3}{4}$ in
2   2 ft 1 in × 5 in
4   2 ft × 3 in
1   1 ft 8 in × 3 in
1   4 ft 5 in × $2\frac{1}{2}$ in

Softwood $\frac{5}{8}$ in
4   13 ft × $1\frac{1}{2}$ in
2   8 ft 4 in × $1\frac{1}{2}$ in

Softwood $\frac{1}{2}$ in
4   3 ft 2 in × 2 in

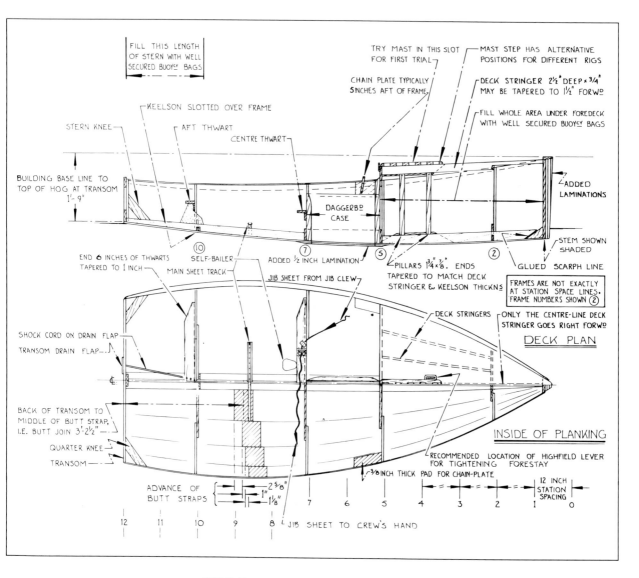

Plan 4.2 Hull section and deck and hull plan.

►KILDA – BUILDING NOTES

The construction of *Kilda* is described in detail in the notes that follow. However, it is difficult to reproduce drawings for a boat of this type at an adequate scale in a book, so large drawings can be purchased for £35 (including packing and postage) from the authors at Linnfield, Cove, Helensburgh, Dunbartonshire, G84 0NS.

Please study the drawings very carefully and read these notes right through before commencing building. To save time some items can be prepared and glued, varnished, etc in batches well before they are required.

Throughout the construction only good quality wood should be used.

It must be free from knots, cracks and blemishes. All frames and transom, hog, keelson, beams, thwarts, mast pillars, mast step and gunwhale cap, also top, bottom and end pieces of dagger-board case, should be of medium-weight hardwood such as mahogany. All screws to be brass, bronze or stainless steel. We used two part epoxy glue produced by Structural Polymer Systems Ltd.

Making the frames and transom

Prepare full-size paper patterns for the parts of each frame from the frame plan (4.3) and table of offsets. Cut out the frame pieces from $\frac{5}{8}$ in thick hardwood by marking round the paper pattern onto the wood. Cut $\frac{1}{16}$ in outside the pencil line. Having cut out a frame part for, say, the frame by station 2 starboard side, use this as a template for the port side.

▶ KILDA – FRAME DIMENSIONS

All measurements in inches

	Distance off centre-line										Distances above top of Hog			
	A	B	C	D	E	F	G	H	J	V	W	X	Y	Z
Frame by Station 2	$1\frac{1}{2}$	4	$5\frac{1}{2}$	$6\frac{1}{2}$	$7\frac{5}{8}$	$8\frac{5}{8}$	$9\frac{1}{2}$	$10\frac{1}{2}$	$11\frac{1}{4}$					
Frame by Station 5	$3\frac{1}{4}$	12	$16\frac{3}{4}$	$19\frac{3}{4}$	$21\frac{3}{4}$	$23\frac{3}{8}$	24	$24\frac{5}{8}$						
Frame by Station 7 See plan 4.4	$3\frac{3}{4}$	17	$21\frac{7}{8}$	$24\frac{5}{8}$	$26\frac{1}{2}$	$27\frac{3}{4}$	$28\frac{1}{2}$				$\frac{1}{8}$	$\frac{3}{8}$	1	$2\frac{1}{8}$
Frame by Station 10	3	$16\frac{7}{8}$	$21\frac{1}{8}$	$24\frac{7}{8}$	$27\frac{3}{8}$	$29\frac{3}{4}$					$\frac{3}{8}$	$\frac{3}{4}$	$1\frac{3}{8}$	$2\frac{1}{4}$
Transom	$2\frac{3}{4}$	$14\frac{3}{4}$	$19\frac{1}{4}$	22	$24\frac{1}{2}$						$\frac{1}{4}$	$\frac{7}{8}$	$1\frac{1}{4}$	$3\frac{1}{8}$

As each piece is made it should be labelled in chalk. If pencil is used, it will not be easy to erase before varnishing and if not erased it will show through the varnish. Label each piece with frame number and side, also forward or aft face. Remember the bottom pieces of each frame extend port and starboard (plan 4.3 only shows one side).

Plane the inner and outer edges of the upper frame piece for one side to the correct shape (comparing regularly with the paper pattern), then use this piece as a template for planing the upper frame piece on the other side to the correct shape.

Now lay all the pieces for one frame on a perfectly flat floor and line them up as shown on plan 4.3, ensuring correct overall depth, width and also the correct overlaps for upper and bottom pieces are obtained.

Now drill and screw the pieces together. Then dismantle the frame, apply glue to the overlaps and reassemble. Repeat this procedure for each frame.

The frames at stations 2 and 10 require to be notched to accept the keelson; this is explained more fully under 'Constructing the keel'. The thwart support beams for the frames at stations 7 and 10 should be made up and screwed and glued to the aft faces of these frames at this stage (see plan 4.3).

Plan 4.3 Frame plan.

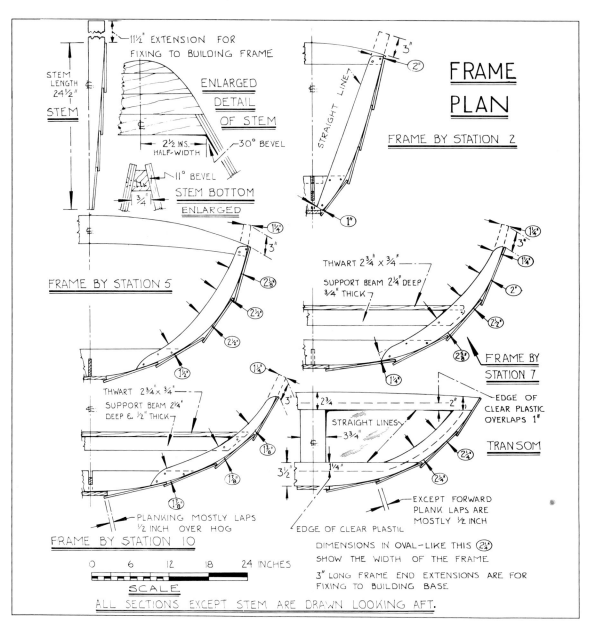

52

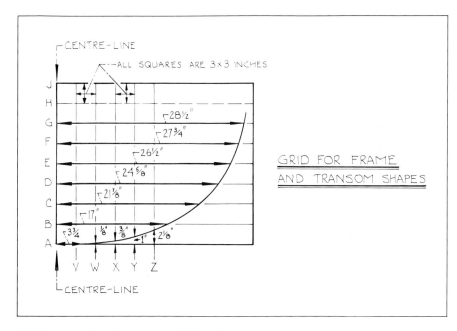

CENTRE-LINE

ALL SQUARES ARE 3×3 INCHES

GRID FOR FRAME
AND TRANSOM SHAPES

Plan 4.4 Grid for frame and
transom shapes.

Setting up frames on building base

To set up a building base, which consists of two heavy timber longitudinal pieces set on edge approximately 3 ft 4 in apart and parallel, first construct a rectangular framework held rigid by diagonals between supports (see plan 4.5). The framework should support the longitudinals so that their top edges will be between 2 ft and 2 ft 6 in above the floor. Now cut longitudinals out of heavy-duty staging-type timber (say 9 in × $1\frac{1}{2}$ in). These must be about 1 ft 6 in longer than the boat. Try setting up the end framework and provisionally clamping the longitudinals in place – now adjust them to ensure that they are level both *longitudinally* and *laterally* in relation to each other. Their top edges must not only be level, they must be perfectly straight. So before setting these pieces up it may be necessary to plane the top edges. Having done this, secure with large bolts or screws and if possible add additional pieces from the framework to ceiling and/or walls for added rigidity. Fit diagonal stiffeners to the building base on the under side of the 9 in × $1\frac{1}{2}$ in pieces, extending from port aft corner to starboard forward corner and starboard aft corner to port forward corner, as seen in plan view.

The next task is to set up the boat frames at the correct positions fore-and-aft *upside down* (the boat is built upside down for ease of planking). Stout cross pieces (typically 4 in × 2 in × at least 5 ft long) are fitted across the building base at frame positions (see plan 4.5). The frames must be at the correct heights in relation to the *building base line*. All frames should have the level of the gunwhale/sheer line marked on. By reference to the drawing on plan 4.5 showing the distance from the building base line to the inverted frame highest point, set up the frames at the correct heights above the building base longitudinals. This will require the use of temporary extension pieces (at all frames except station 2 and stem) which should be attached to each frame end where there is a surplus of timber (see plan 4.3) for this purpose.

Plan 4.5 Hog, deck beams and building base.

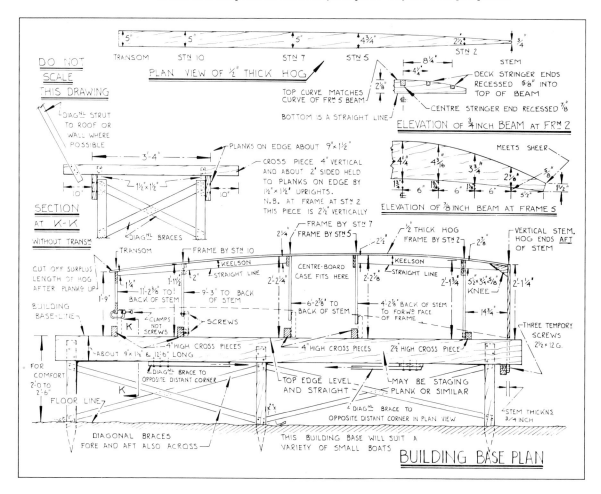

The stem, which is in effect a frame located right forward, is a solid piece of wood. It is bevelled on each side *before* being erected. The bevel angle is 11 degrees at the bottom for the lowest plank, ie the garboard. The bevel angle gradually changes to 30 degrees at the top. No other frame is bevelled, not even the transom.

Constructing the keel

Having set up the frames, cut out the hog and keelson pieces by reference to the dimensions on the drawings in plan 4.5. The hog is 11 ft 6 in × $5\frac{1}{2}$ in × $\frac{1}{2}$ in tapered at the forward end as shown on the plan and the keelson pieces are $\frac{5}{8}$ in timber, cut to the drawing dimensions.

The hog is fitted in place over each frame ensuring each one is vertical; it is screwed (with $1\frac{1}{2}$ in, 10-gauge screws) and glued at each frame. At the stem the hog is butt-jointed to the aft side of the stem and an additional knee is required to ensure a good strong fit (see plan 4.5). This knee may be cut when the hog is provisionally fitted so that its exact shape can be obtained. When cutting the forward keelson piece ensure that the forward end will scarf onto the stem knee satisfactorily.

The frames at stations 2 and 10 require to be notched (also keelson pieces at these points) 'egg box' style so that the keelson will lie flush against the hog (see plan 4.6). The keelson pieces may require further planing and fitting to lie flush against the hog. The edge of the keelson next to the hog is notched to half depth first, and then the floor of the frame is notched sufficiently deep to allow the keelson to lie flush against the hog. After fitting the keelson, restore the strength of the frames at stations 2 and 10 by gluing $\frac{5}{8}$ in thick doublers over. Keelson pieces are butt jointed (screw and glue) to the centre-line of the bottom pieces at frame stations 5, 7 and transom.

Plan 4.6 Frame-keelson join.

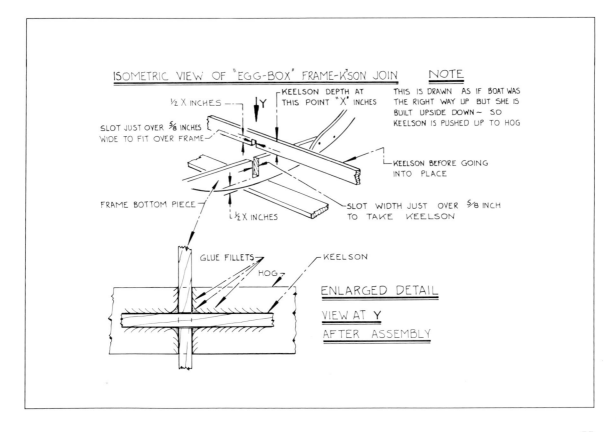

ISOMETRIC VIEW OF "EGG-BOX" FRAME-K'SON JOIN   NOTE

½ X INCHES

KEELSON DEPTH AT THIS POINT "X" INCHES

THIS IS DRAWN AS IF BOAT WAS THE RIGHT WAY UP BUT SHE IS BUILT UPSIDE DOWN ~ SO KEELSON IS PUSHED UP TO HOG

SLOT JUST OVER $\frac{5}{8}$ INCHES WIDE TO FIT OVER FRAME

KEELSON BEFORE GOING INTO PLACE

FRAME BOTTOM PIECE

1 ½ X INCHES

SLOT WIDTH JUST OVER $\frac{5}{8}$ INCH TO TAKE KEELSON

GLUE FILLETS

HOG

KEELSON

ENLARGED DETAIL

VIEW AT Y

AFTER ASSEMBLY

55

Marking, cutting and fitting planks

For this operation refer to plan 4.7 of plank shapes and layout.

Firstly cut one of the 8 ft × 4 ft pieces of 6 mm marine ply in half, giving two half pieces 4 ft × 4 ft. Place one whole piece and one half piece end to end in line on a flat floor, with the grain running the same way, ie along the length. Clamp wood battens to the ply to ensure the pieces do not move relative to each other. Now using the dimensions on the plank plan (4.7) and table of offsets mark out all the plank shapes for one side of the boat. Cut the garboard strake to shape allowing a margin of $\frac{1}{16}$ in for fairing and planing. Using surplus ply cut the butt strap, which laps 3 in

Plan 4.7 Plank shapes and butt straps:

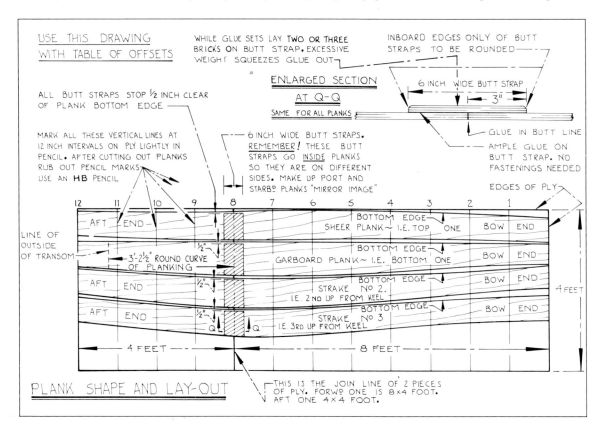

USE THIS DRAWING WITH TABLE OF OFFSETS

WHILE GLUE SETS LAY TWO OR THREE BRICKS ON BUTT STRAP. EXCESSIVE WEIGHT SQUEEZES GLUE OUT

INBOARD EDGES ONLY OF BUTT STRAPS TO BE ROUNDED

ENLARGED SECTION AT Q-Q

6 INCH WIDE BUTT STRAP

SAME FOR ALL PLANKS

3"

ALL BUTT STRAPS STOP ½ INCH CLEAR OF PLANK BOTTOM EDGE

GLUE IN BUTT LINE

MARK ALL THESE VERTICAL LINES AT 12 INCH INTERVALS ON PLY LIGHTLY IN PENCIL. AFTER CUTTING OUT PLANKS RUB OUT PENCIL MARKS. USE AN HB PENCIL

6 INCH WIDE BUTT STRAPS. REMEMBER! THESE BUTT STRAPS GO INSIDE PLANKS SO THEY ARE ON DIFFERENT SIDES. MAKE UP PORT AND STARBD PLANKS "MIRROR IMAGE"

AMPLE GLUE ON BUTT STRAP. NO FASTENINGS NEEDED

EDGES OF PLY

12 11 10 9 8 7 6 5 4 3 2 1

AFT END

BOTTOM EDGE
SHEER PLANK ~ I.E. TOP ONE   BOW END

LINE OF OUTSIDE OF TRANSOM

½"

3'-2½" ROUND CURVE OF PLANKING

BOTTOM EDGE
GARBOARD PLANK ~ I.E. BOTTOM ONE   BOW END

AFT END

½"

BOTTOM EDGE
STRAKE No 2.
I.E. 2ND UP FROM KEEL   BOW END

4 FEET

AFT END

½"

BOTTOM EDGE
STRAKE No 3
I.E. 3RD UP FROM KEEL   BOW END

Q   Q

4 FEET

8 FEET

PLANK SHAPE AND LAY-OUT

THIS IS THE JOIN LINE OF 2 PIECES OF PLY. FORWD ONE IS 8×4 FOOT. AFT ONE 4×4 FOOT.

either side (ie it is 6 in wide) of the butt joint. Round the fore and aft edges as shown in the enlarged section Q–Q on plan 4.7. The butt strap should be $\frac{1}{2}$ in clear of the *lower* edge of the plank at every plank to allow for the standard lap of the planks. Place the two pieces of the first garboard on the floor and butt joint tight together and glue the butt strap in place. Cover the glued join in polythene and weight down well with bricks or similar to ensure a good tight joint. When the joint has set, plane and finish the plank edges.

▶ KILDA – PLANK DIMENSIONS

All measurements in inches from top edge of ply (Plan 4.7)

THIS END IS THE STERN   THIS END IS THE BOW

Measurement points (not frame lines)		12	11	10	9	8	7	6	5	4	3	2	1	0
Sheer strake ie top plank	Bottom Edge	$\frac{5}{8}$	$\frac{3}{4}$	$\frac{3}{4}$	$\frac{3}{4}$	$\frac{5}{8}$	$\frac{3}{8}$	$\frac{1}{8}$	$\frac{1}{8}$	$\frac{3}{8}$	$\frac{3}{4}$	1	$1\frac{1}{2}$	$2\frac{1}{8}$
	Top Edge	8	$8\frac{1}{2}$	$8\frac{3}{4}$	9	$9\frac{1}{8}$	9	$8\frac{7}{8}$	$8\frac{3}{4}$	$8\frac{3}{4}$	$8\frac{3}{4}$	$8\frac{3}{4}$	9	$9\frac{3}{8}$
Garboard strake ie bottom plank	Bottom Edge	$9\frac{5}{8}$	$9\frac{5}{8}$	$9\frac{5}{8}$	$9\frac{5}{8}$	$9\frac{5}{8}$	$9\frac{5}{8}$	$9\frac{5}{8}$	$9\frac{5}{8}$	$9\frac{5}{8}$	$9\frac{3}{4}$	$9\frac{7}{8}$	$9\frac{7}{8}$	10
	Top Edge	$17\frac{1}{8}$	$17\frac{3}{4}$	$18\frac{5}{8}$	$19\frac{1}{4}$	$19\frac{3}{4}$	$19\frac{7}{8}$	$19\frac{3}{4}$	$19\frac{1}{8}$	$18\frac{1}{2}$	$17\frac{7}{8}$	$16\frac{5}{8}$	$16\frac{1}{4}$	$15\frac{7}{8}$
No 2 Strake ie No. 2 plank counting up from keel	Bottom Edge	$17\frac{3}{4}$	$18\frac{1}{2}$	$19\frac{1}{4}$	$19\frac{7}{8}$	$20\frac{1}{4}$	$20\frac{1}{4}$	20	$19\frac{5}{8}$	$19\frac{1}{4}$	$18\frac{7}{8}$	$18\frac{1}{4}$	$17\frac{7}{8}$	$16\frac{3}{8}$
	Top Edge	$25\frac{1}{8}$	$26\frac{1}{2}$	$27\frac{5}{8}$	$28\frac{5}{8}$	$29\frac{1}{4}$	$29\frac{1}{4}$	$28\frac{3}{4}$	$27\frac{7}{8}$	$26\frac{7}{8}$	$25\frac{7}{8}$	$24\frac{5}{8}$	$23\frac{5}{8}$	$23\frac{1}{8}$
No 3 Strake ie No. 3 plank counting up from keel	Bottom Edge	$26\frac{1}{8}$	$27\frac{1}{8}$	$28\frac{1}{4}$	$29\frac{1}{8}$	$29\frac{3}{4}$	$29\frac{5}{8}$	29	$28\frac{3}{4}$	$27\frac{7}{8}$	27	$26\frac{1}{8}$	$25\frac{1}{2}$	25
	Top Edge	$33\frac{5}{8}$	$34\frac{5}{8}$	$35\frac{3}{4}$	$36\frac{7}{8}$	$37\frac{3}{4}$	$37\frac{5}{8}$	$37\frac{1}{8}$	$36\frac{1}{8}$	$35\frac{1}{8}$	$34\frac{1}{4}$	$33\frac{3}{8}$	33	$32\frac{5}{8}$

Before fitting the planks cut out 12 wooden rectangular clamps which, with the use of wedges, will hold the plank laps/edges tightly in place (see plan 4.8).

Before fitting the first garboard strake in place use it as a template for the other garboard strake. Remember to make the planks left- and right-handed. In each case when the first of a pair of strakes is cut to shape and joined, it is used as a template for the other plank of the pair.

With the use of wood clamps, also carpenter's clamps, weights and perhaps struts to the ceiling, fit the first garboard in place. Locate the garboard plank in the fore-and-aft direction with the centre of the butt 3 ft $2\frac{1}{2}$ in from the aft side of the transom and the edge of the plank overlapping the hog by $\frac{1}{2}$ in amidships and at the transom. Towards the bow the plank twists to meet the stem. Consequently the lap at the hog is more open, requiring a large glue fillet as described below.

Using stiffened glue mixture (microfibres added to S.P. Systems resin and hardener), fillet-glue the edge of the plank to the bottom of the hog. The garboard strake has the most twist of all the planks, therefore gluing is very important here. When the glue has set release the clamps slightly to allow screwing and gluing of the plank to the stem and frames. This plank should have screws at every frame because of the twist. When the glue has set repeat the whole procedure for the other garboard strake.

Now cut out the first No 2 strake and try fitting the forward part of the plank in place. The edge of the garboard may need planing to ensure the second plank lies snugly against it. The outer edge of the garboard must be slightly bevelled at the stem to allow a better land for the next plank. Then try the aft part of the plank. If the butt joint is not quite right

Plan 4.8 Use of clamps and wedges for gluing planks.

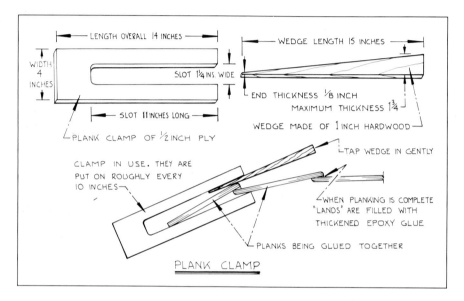

Photo 4.2 Fitting a garboard plank. Note also how the frames are set up on the building base.

(edge to edge), adjustment of the angle of the butt joint can be made at this point by cutting a thin triangular sliver of ply from the butt edge to achieve a satisfactory joint. Now remove both parts of the plank and glue the butt strap as for the garboard. When set use the plank as a template for the other one of the pair.

Now fix the plank in place using the specially made wood rectangular clamps, etc (these wooden clamps are now vital at the laps). Firstly glue all along the lap by slackening and refixing the plank progressively along its whole length. Because the plank edges are not much bevelled it is important to ensure that the garboard edge is well saturated with glue to ensure a good, strong, tight lap. When the glue has set use two screws at the stem and one at the frame (station 2) only. Screw and glue the plank fully, using only small amounts of glue to attach the plank where it just touches each frame. Light clamping at the plank edges onto

Photo 4.3 Fitting a No 2 strake. Note the use of clamps.

frames is alright, but not too tight as this will distort the edge for the next lap. Having glued the butt strap for the second No 2 strake, now fair this plank and fit it. It may be necessary to support the plank laps with wood struts from the floor at their underside to ensure a close fit without distortion of hull shape. When carrying out the second lot of gluing of the No 2 strakes, fillet glue into the lap (tidying away any surplus).

The butt joints and butt straps should be staggered as shown on plan 4.2. Note that not all the distances between the butts are equal and the garboard butt is furthest aft.

Now proceed with construction and fitting of the No 3 strakes and sheer strakes as described for the No 2 strake. The same two-stage gluing process is followed: *firstly* glue lap and clamp the plank in position; and when set, *secondly* glue plank to frames and fillet the plank lap fully. When fitting the butt straps to these planks the angle of the butt join can be adjusted if preliminary pre-glue fitting of the two parts of the plank to the hull shows this is necessary to achieve a fair line along the

Photo 4.4 Fitting a No 3 strake, viewed from inside the hull.

Photo 4.5 Clamping a plank at the stem while the glue sets.

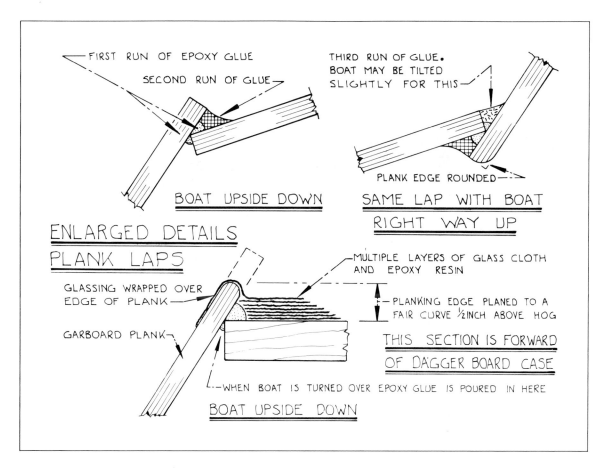

FIRST RUN OF EPOXY GLUE

SECOND RUN OF GLUE

THIRD RUN OF GLUE.
BOAT MAY BE TILTED
SLIGHTLY FOR THIS

PLANK EDGE ROUNDED

BOAT UPSIDE DOWN

SAME LAP WITH BOAT
RIGHT WAY UP

ENLARGED DETAILS
PLANK LAPS

GLASSING WRAPPED OVER
EDGE OF PLANK

GARBOARD PLANK

MULTIPLE LAYERS OF GLASS CLOTH
AND EPOXY RESIN

PLANKING EDGE PLANED TO A
FAIR CURVE ½ INCH ABOVE HOG

THIS SECTION IS FORWARD
OF DAGGER BOARD CASE

WHEN BOAT IS TURNED OVER EPOXY GLUE IS POURED IN HERE

BOAT UPSIDE DOWN

plank edges. It should not be necessary to use screws for attachment of No 3 strakes and the sheer strakes as they have less twist than the first two planks, but it will still be necessary to bevel the upper edge of the previous plank near the bow before placing the next plank in position to achieve a good tight lap here.

When all the planks are glued in position, additional filleting with glue is carried out at the laps to achieve a really good fillet (see plan 4.9). When the glue has fully set the excess plank lengths at stem and transom can be carefully trimmed off.

Plan 4.9 Use of glue and glass cloth to seal plank laps.

Photo 4.6 Softwood laminations fitted to the stem.

Laminating the stem/bow

The stem laminations are straight-sided, two to three in number depending on the thickness of the wood available. Their outer edges cover all the plank ends so the first one is made by holding a piece of wood on the stem and drawing round it. They are glued on in turn, and shaped with a plane or Surform to give an attractive rounded stem (see plan 4.3).

61

Finishing the keel externally

The next task is to plane away the surplus of the garboard planks at the forward end of the keel. These edges of the garboards should still extend about $\frac{1}{2}$ in beyond the hog so as not to weaken the important glue fillet at this point. Ensure the lower garboard edges are in line with one another when the hull is viewed from the side and front. Now cut a piece of $\frac{1}{2}$ in hardwood plank to shape, extending on the outside of the hog from forward of station 5 to aft of station 7, a distance of about 2 ft 6 in. This forms an additional lamination for extra strength where the dagger-board slot will later be cut in the bottom of the boat. This piece will have to be carefully shaped to fit on the hog between the garboard plank edges and glue fillets. It should be fully tapered over 3 in at each end to reduce turbulence.

Next cut about three lengths of 2 in glass cloth tape to extend from station 7 to the stem, and epoxy glue them in place. These will form a bed for the additional lamination from stations 5 to 7 which is then weighted down in position with bricks or similar. Further shorter lengths of glass cloth tape are epoxied in position from the forward end of the lamination at station 5 right forward to the stem, so as to half fill the whole length of the channel between the garboard edges and lap those edges to produce a strong, even keel (see plan 4.9).

The gaps at the transom between the plank ends and the transom frame are now filled with small hardwood wedges held in place with copious glue made too thick to run by adding filler (see plan 4.10). The wedges should protrude roughly $\frac{1}{8}$ in aft of the transom. When the glue is solid but not rock hard, the protruding pieces of wedge are planed off flush

Plan 4.10 Use of wedges between planks and transom frame.

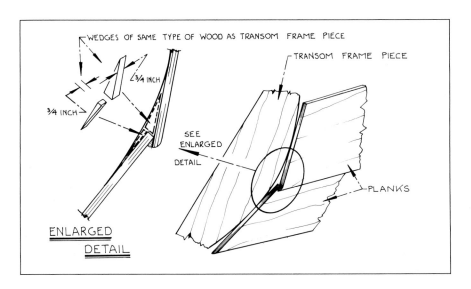

WEDGES OF SAME TYPE OF WOOD AS TRANSOM FRAME PIECE

TRANSOM FRAME PIECE

3/4 INCH

3/4 INCH

SEE ENLARGED DETAIL

PLANKS

ENLARGED DETAIL

with the aft face of the transom. NOTE Excess glue should be wiped off with a rag before it hardens. Where glue has to be faired off, this should be done when the glue has set to the consistency of a very hard cheese and before it becomes rock solid.

Next the deck beam at the frame by station 5 is cut (see dimensions on plan 4.5) and screwed and glued in place to the top ends of the frame.

The hull can now be removed from the building base and the surplus material at the frame ends rounded off. The thwarts or seats are cut and shaped to the dimensions shown on plans 4.2 and 4.3 and screwed and glued in position (for detail of aft thwart see plan 4.11). The ends of the thwarts do not touch the planking.

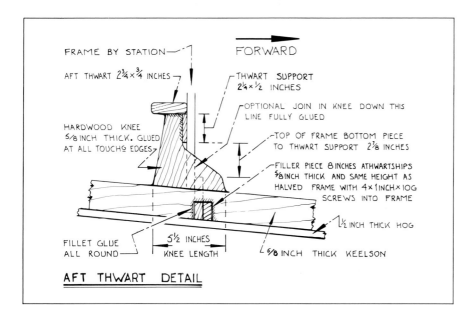

Plan 4.11 Aft thwart.

Making the dagger-board case

The dagger-board case is constructed using hardwood spacers at the fore and aft ends and ply sides (from surplus after planks are cut). The lower edges of the sides are of hardwood or softwood and for stiffeners at upper edges hardwood is used. They are cut to the dimensions on plan 4.13 then screwed and glued together. This task can be carried out at an earlier stage to fit in with other gluing sessions. When shaped and finished, the box is fitted *exactly* in position. This is best done by placing a thin, tight string or wire over the centre-line of the boat from centre top of stem to centre top of transom and lining the case up. Draw round the case on the hog and mark its position on the thwarts and frame (station 5) deck beam. Remove the case and plot the internal dimensions of the dagger-board case slot on the hog. Now mark out on the hog a section

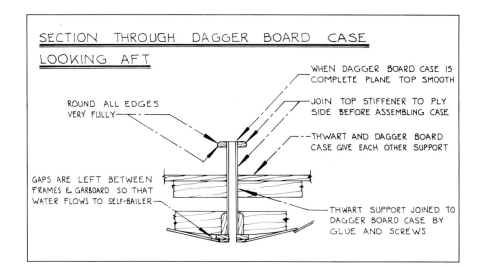

Plan 4.12 Dagger-board case.

Plan 4.13 Dagger-board and dagger-board case details.

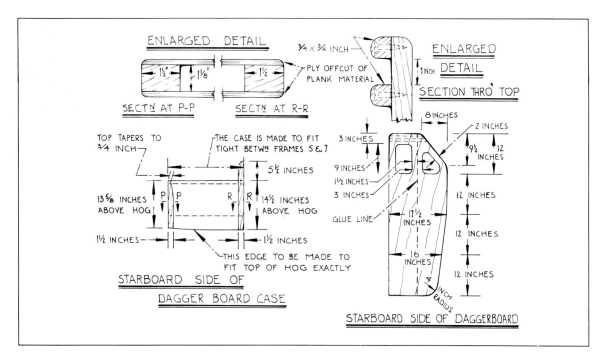

similar to, but $\frac{1}{8}$ in larger all round than, the eventual dagger-board shape (see plan 4.16). Mark this section on the centre-line and within the dimensions of the dagger-board case slot. Ensure that the hull is well supported beneath and at the sides, climb gently inside the hull and with drill and jig saw cut out the hole for the dagger-board, keeping the saw blade $\frac{1}{16}$ in inside the line for later fairing.

Four screw holes for 10- or 12-gauge screws are now drilled down through the hog (and countersunk from underneath) either side of the slot. The dagger-board case is placed in position again and these four holes for the securing screws are extended by drilling upwards into the sides of the case (see plan 4.19). The case is also fixed vertically by screws at the station 5 deck beam and the vertical part of the station 7 thwart. The case can now be glued (with thickened glue) and screwed in place. It is particularly important to ensure that the join between the hog and the dagger-board case is watertight. Use plenty of glue, well spread, at this point to achieve a really watertight seal.

Photo 4.7 Dagger-board case (inverted) ready for fitting.

Photo 4.8 Hole cut in the hog for the dagger-board.

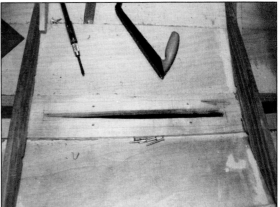

Making the gunwhale rubbing strakes

While work is proceeding on the thwarts and dagger-board case, construction of the gunwhale rubbing strakes can also be going forward. These are constructed of $1\frac{1}{2}$ in $\times$ $\frac{5}{8}$ in softwood which should be free of knots, and each piece must be 13 ft long. Each piece is planed smooth on all faces and the first piece on one side is clamped in place along the sheer line. Glue is applied to the *outer face* of the first piece and the second piece is clamped accurately on top. When the glue has set remove the clamps and store the rubbing strake by tying it up tightly like a bow with string from one end to the other so that the curve of the wood is retained. Now repeat the process for the rubbing strake on the other side. When the glue is set, both rubbing strakes should be planed and finished: the forward ends of the rubbing strakes are tapered to approximately $\frac{7}{8}$ in in thickness and $\frac{7}{8}$ in in depth. A further lamination is then prepared which extends from 1 ft forward of station 5 to 6 in forward of the transom. The ends of these laminations are tapered to $\frac{1}{8}$ in thick.

The gunwhale rubbing strakes can now be glued to the sheer planks. Using clamps at 18 in intervals both rubbing strakes are glued on at the same time in order to avoid pulling the hull out of shape. To reduce the number of clamps needed and to ensure that the aft ends are well glued, the rubbing strake should be run beyond the transom at least 4 in and

Photo 4.9 Fitting a rubbing strake.

better still about 8 in. These two extensions should be tied together tightly using a Spanish windlass to pull them together. When the glue has set the additional (third) shorter lamination can be glued and clamped in position as described above. Again both sides should be glued on at the same time. When the glue has set the upper surface of each rubbing strake is planed smooth to accept the capping pieces. Care should be taken when planing not to overdo this and change the sheer line.

Before the capping pieces are prepared the wood pads for the chain-plates are cut from $\frac{3}{8}$ in hardwood (dimensions: 9 in horizontal × 7 in vertical or to fit chain-plates). They are planed and finished all over, then glued in position aft of station 5 as shown on plans 4.2 and 4.18. The edges must be well rounded and two clamps each are needed to hold them in place while the glue sets.

The gunwhale rubbing strake capping pieces are made in sections from two pieces 7 ft × 4 in × $\frac{1}{4}$ in and two pieces 5 ft × 4 in × $\frac{1}{4}$ in hardwood. The sections from station 5 to the transom are glued permanently in position whereas the forward sections to the bow will be removable and are used to secure the PVC foredeck (see plan 4.18).

Take one of the 7 ft pieces and place one end over the rubbing strake at station 5 and manoeuvre it into a position where it covers the softwood rubber and the sheer strake ply edge as far aft as possible (probably just aft of the butt strap, the edge of which it must cover). Now pencil on the underside the shape of the inner and outer edge and make a diagonal scarfed joint with the next piece to be fitted further aft. Cut this piece out and clamp it in position. Repeat the procedure and cut out the section to the stern. The two pieces can now be glued and clamped in position on one side over the rubbing strake between station 5 and the stern. Repeat the procedure for the other side and round all edges of the capping when the glue has set. It is alright to do one side at a time here, and plenty of clamps are required.

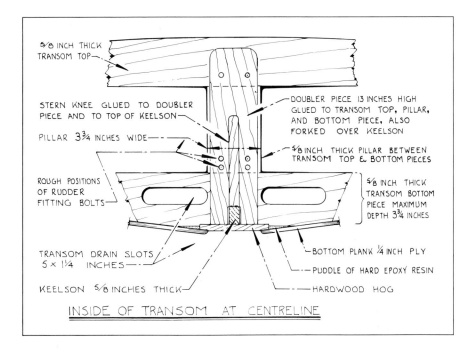

Plan 4.14 Inside of transom.

67

Drain slots are cut in the lower part of the transom bottom piece to the dimensions and positions shown on plan 4.14. A hardwood pillar (see plan) is glued between the centre of the base of the transom bottom piece and the transom top; this takes the rudder fittings later.

A doubler should be made up, dimensions 13 in × 3¾ in × ⅝ in, for gluing to the transom bottom piece, pillar and top. It is slotted or forked over the keelson at its base. This provides additional thickness and strength for attachment of the rudder fittings.

A small triangular hardwood knee is prepared (10 in × 2½ in × ⅝ in) and glued in position between the aft end of the keelson and the centre of the pillar (see plan 4.2). Quarter knees are made up as shown on the plan for fitting between the transom top and the upper edge of the sheer strake (see plan 4.15).

Plan 4.15 Quarter knee.

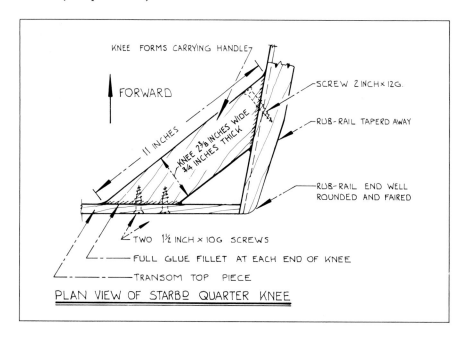

While work is proceeding on the various foregoing items, in order to cut down the number of gluing sessions the dagger-board, mast support structure and deck stringers can be made.

Making the dagger-board

The dagger-board is made up to the dimensions and the section shown on plans 4.13 and 4.16. A good wood for this is yellow pine, ⅞ in thick. It is likely that you will have to glue two longitudinal sections edge to edge. To line up the edges when gluing, it is helpful to have three locating pins in the edge made from screws partially screwed into one edge. Their

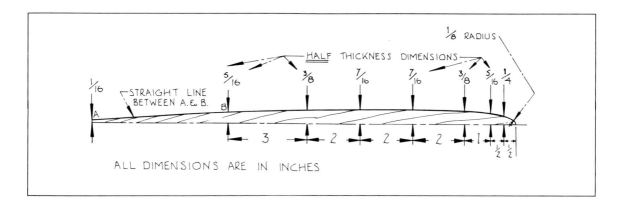

heads are sawn off and the shanks of the screws fit in holes drilled in the opposite edge. The accurate placing of these holes is important, and this can be done by placing the edge with the locating pins in place firmly against the opposite edge so that the pins make an impression in it to indicate where the locating holes should be drilled. The two pieces should also have their lightening holes cut in them (above the waterline) as shown on plan 4.13. These holes will help with gluing and clamping the two pieces edge to edge which is done next. A Spanish windlass of thin rope right round the board will also help draw the edges tight together.

Plan 4.16 Dagger-board section. The dagger-board is given a 'wing' section for good performance to windward. Before beginning to make the board this shape, pencil the centre-line on all four edges. Make up a template to the shape of this section, then saw, chisel and plane the dagger-board until it fits the template.

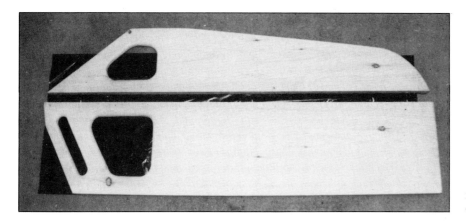

Photo 4.10 Dagger-board in two sections ready for gluing together.

When the glue has set work can begin on shaping the board to the section shown on plan 4.16.

Two short wood pieces are screwed and glued to the top of the board as extra handholds and to prevent the board from going down too far. A hole is drilled between them to accept a removable pin with an eye, which is attached to the dagger-board case with cord so that the board can be held in the fully down position.

An additional deck beam (see plan 4.5) with cambered top is now prepared for attachment to the frame by station 2 and screwed and glued in position.

Making the mast support structure

The mast support structure comprises two hardwood pillars and a softwood stringer on edge which is notched with screw and glue into the station 5 deck beam, notched into the station 2 deck beam and butt-glued to the inner face of the stem section. The dimensions of the pillars and stringer are shown on plan 4.17 but it is important that the pillars should be a tight fit where shown between the stringer and the upper

Plan 4.17 Mast step and support structure.

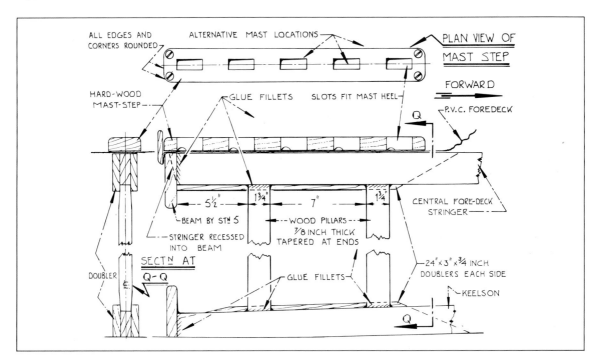

edge of the keelson. In addition, there are upper and lower softwood doublers on edge (dimensions 2 ft × 3 in × $\frac{3}{4}$ in) in way of the mast support area. The upper doublers are butted onto the station 5 deck beam with upper edges level with the stringer and lower edges overlapping the uprights by $\frac{1}{2}$ in or so. All this structure can now be screwed, glued and clamped in position.

The foredeck

The PVC foredeck is supported not only by the centre-line stringer but

Photo 4.11 Hull during painting and varnishing. Note the arrangement of the foredeck support beams.

also by four longitudinal softwood pieces on edge between the stations 2 and 5 deck beams, positioned as shown on plan 4.2. These additional stringers are tapered in depth from approximately half their length to their forward ends. They are notched into the deck beam at the station 2 frame and notched (see plan 4.2) into the deck beam at the station 5 frame. These can now be clamped and glued into position.

The foredeck should be made from a piece of PVC cut considerably oversize so that it will 'lap' the aft side of the station 5 deck beam and cover the top of the stem. At this stage it should extend well over the gunwhales, and holes are cut below the gunwhales at approximately 9 in spacing so that when the PVC is placed over the foredeck area it can be laced tight with rope passed through the holes and back and forth under the boat. Having fitted it approximately, it can now be removed and put aside for permanent fixing later.

The next job is to make the forward gunwhale rubbing strake capping pieces. These are made from the two 5 ft × 4 in × $\frac{1}{4}$ in hardwood pieces referred to earlier. The pieces are placed over the gunwhale rubbing strakes and sheer plank edges from station 5 forward to the stem, ensuring that the plank edges and rubbing strakes are fully covered. The aft end butts right up against the forward end of the amidships capping piece at station 5. Now clamp each piece in place and pencil mark round its outer shape underneath. On the inboard side the fair line of the forward end of the amidships capping piece, which covers the edge of the chain-plate doublers, should continue forward to the stem. These forward capping pieces are now secured with 10-gauge *screws only* at 4 in intervals into the centre-line of the gunwhale rubbing strake. The capping pieces are cut to shape and the top edges rounded.

A hardwood capping piece to cover the top of the stem is made up so that it fits exactly over the stem and between the forward ends of the gunwhale rubbing strake capping pieces. This is screwed in position with two 10-gauge screws and then removed and stored for use later.

Mainsheet traveller

An athwartships piece is made of hardwood for fitting over the hog and lower planks to take the track for the traveller as shown on the plan 4.2. It is located over the forward end of the garboard butt straps and notched over the keelson. This piece is glued and screwed in place using four screws inserted upwards through the underside of the boat (care is needed in lining these up accurately by drilling downwards after taking the piece of hardwood out of the way). The mainsheet track is screwed in place then removed and stored prior to internal varnishing/painting.

Self-bailers

We would recommend that two Holt-Allen or similar stainless steel dinghy self-bailers are fitted in the garboards either side between the frame at station 7 and the butt strap. The holes for these should be accurately cut before painting, etc, so that the ply edges can be well covered with paint or varnish. Sealing compound should be used when fitting the bailers.

Finishing, painting, etc

The boat should now be turned upside down again so that the underside of the gunwhale rubbing strakes can be planed, shaped and sanded to give a nice rounded appearance. (See detail sections on plan 4.18.)

All plank laps and the keel area should be carefully sanded and finished to remove surplus epoxy and give a smooth finish. Laps and butt joints can be brush-coated with epoxy using a disposable paint brush. Inside, ply laps should be fillet glued, then sanded and finished and surplus epoxy removed.

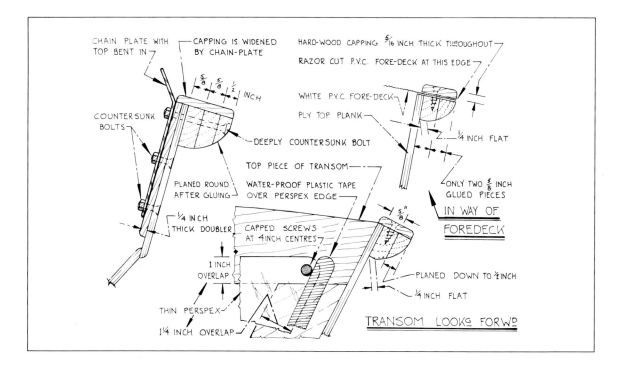

The boat should now be turned on her side for trial fitting of the dagger-board. Both board and slot will probably require further gradual filing and planing to achieve a reasonable fit. We used epoxy glue to proof the inside of the dagger-board case, but several coats of paint or varnish would do instead. This could be done by using an ordinary brush at the construction stage or with the use of absorbent cloth on a long stick when the boat is nearly complete.

We found that, in order to ease lowering and raising of the dagger-board, a short length of heavy duty rubber hose (as used in car cooling systems) was helpful. A length of hose $1\frac{1}{4}$ in long is cut and forced down inside the casing at the aft end.

When building the prototype, we chose to paint the outside of the hull

Plan 4.18 Chain-plate, rubber strake and transom details.

and varnish inside. If this procedure is followed then two coats of marine primer, two coats of marine undercoat and one or more coats of marine enamel are required. The first coat of primer is thinned as per manufacturer's instructions and any filling required can be carried out thereafter. If varnishing the inside, at least five coats are required, the first being thinned as per manufacturer's instructions.

PVC foredeck covering

The PVC can now be secured over the foredeck area. The same procedure as used for provisional fitting (described above) is repeated, with the PVC being lashed down tight and great care being taken to avoid any wrinkles. The aft end of the PVC should be trimmed at the gunwhales and then the gunwhale rubbing strake capping pieces are screwed in place over the PVC. Two small hardwood break-waters should be made up which should project about $\frac{3}{4}$ in above the deck. These are used to attach the PVC to the aft face of the deck beam at station 5 (see plan 4.17) and they therefore have curved top and bottom edges to match the camber of the deck beam. The edges of the PVC at the gunwhales are trimmed neatly from underneath using a Stanley knife or similar.

Transom covering

This is made of heavy-duty clear plastic of the type used for sail windows, etc. It covers the holes in the transom and is cut in one section. It is fixed on the aft face of the transom before the rudder fittings and is secured by screws and cup washers along its upper edge into the transom top (see plan 4.18). The other edges are held with waterproof tape to the transom bottom and side pieces. Alternatively the transom holes may be covered with light plywood.

Transom drain flaps

These are cut from Perspex or ply and go over the transom drain holes described earlier. They must overlap 1 in all round and sticky-backed rubber strip is used to improve the seal. The two flaps should be joined by a short piece of Terylene webbing to which they are bolted, the $\frac{3}{16}$ in diameter bolts being countersunk on the inside. The flaps should each have a hole drilled fairly centrally for the attachment of shock cord. The flaps are then held by screws through the webbing into the transom bottom piece. These 8-gauge screws should be placed fairly close to the inside edge of the Perspex to help prevent sag.

Rudder

We bought a purpose-made aluminium alloy dinghy rudder box and tiller, complete with extension and fittings. The wooden box which we used on our previous dinghy, *Longa* (see Chapter 3), is also suitable for *Kilda*. The rudder for *Kilda* should be of similar dimensions but 4 in deeper. Suitable fittings (gudgeons and pintles) can be obtained from dinghy fitting suppliers.

Rig

Kilda is well suited to a high-aspect efficient dinghy racing rig of about 90 sq ft (main and jib). Because the mast is deck-stepped we have fitted lower shrouds to stiffen it. We used a quick rigging system which includes a Highfield lever with a hook on the end. It is on the side of the mast step (see plan 4.2) and a loop on the forestay extension wire is secured to the hook. The extension wire goes under a roller on the stem-head fitting which, like the chain-plates, can be obtained from dinghy fitting suppliers. The stem-head fitting must be of the type which extends down the forward face of the stem. The chain-plates should be of the type having three securing bolts; the uppermost bolt is inserted through the gunwhale rubbing strake on each side and is well countersunk (see plan 4.18).

The jib sheets are led through bullseye fairleads and cam cleats, one

Plan 4.19 Centre thwart.

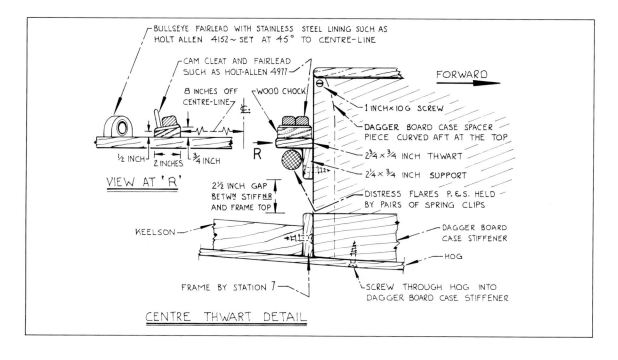

CENTRE THWART DETAIL

of each being situated either side of the dagger-board case on top of the forward thwart (plan 4.19). The precise positions and angle of these fittings should be carefully thought out to suit the rig to be used, required sheeting angle and the need for the crew to be able to work the sheets from the weather side of the boat (see plan 4.2).

Buoyancy

Ample buoyancy is essential. At the forward end of the boat use three large buoyancy bags (150 lb (63 kg) flotation each), plus some additional smaller bags well secured under the foredeck. At the aft end of the boat use two long bags secured to either side of the aft thwart (35 lb (16 kg) flotation each), two bags (one either side of the boat) secured fore-and-aft between the thwart and the transom (40 lb (18 kg) flotation each), and a further large bag (150 lb (63 kg) flotation) secured athwartships between these, or the equivalent.

Miscellaneous

Toestraps made from polyester webbing are made up to run from the transom under the thwarts to the station 5 frame. They are screwed strongly to the forward face of the station 5 frame and have loops stitched in at their aft ends. They are tightly lashed with $\frac{1}{8}$ in line (four turns) through a hole drilled in the keelson near the transom.

Liberal use of non-slip material (Tread-Strip or similar) is essential internally on the garboards and No 2 strakes and is desirable also on the No 3 strakes.

CHAPTER 5
Punto 9 feet 3 inches overall

This boat was designed to be very simple, adaptable and attractive to look at. She can be used for fishing, for teaching children to row, for sailing in estuaries and on lakes, and as a yacht's tender. She will particularly appeal to anyone who is finding that inflatable dinghies are too expensive, hard to row, especially in windy conditions, and are too easily damaged and too often stolen.

Construction is simple and sturdy, while the materials used are particularly inexpensive, even by the standards of the boats in this book of low-price craft.

Punto *was designed and built by a friend of ours, David Ryder-Turner, and what follows is his account of how this boat came into being and the main construction principles involved.*

'It was the last race of the autumn Frostbite series, and four of us were

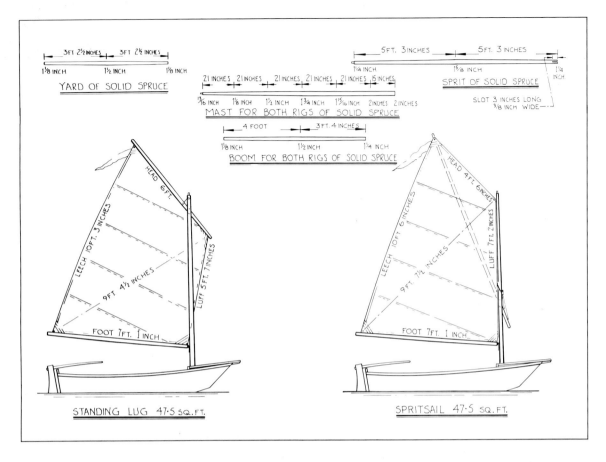

Plan 5.1 Alternative rigs.

going out to our yacht in a rubber dinghy. The rain came down, the sea got up and soon more water was coming in over the bow than was going out over the stern. It was obvious at the half-way mark that we weren't going to reach the cruiser, so we boarded a yacht, emptied the inflatable and got back in again. Going ashore after the race was no better.

Talking it over a few days later, we agreed that there was a need for a tender that could carry four people and their gear, could be dragged up and down a beach with little damage to itself, and could be left on moorings over a weekend. It also had to avoid that curse of inflatables: the Friday evening when the crew arrive to find it has deflated and the pump has been left at home. She must row and tow well. She must perform well with an outboard and have some pretence at sailing ability. We also wanted a boat that was easy and cheap to build with no complex joints. She also had to look good.

For the building material I chose wood since it is cheap and is easily obtained. As a basis of construction, the bottom of the boat is made from a single sheet of 8 ft × 4 ft marine plywood, the sides out of 6 in × ½ in white pine and the frames of 3 in × 1 in white pine. All of these items are readily available. Other timber for thwarts, gunwhale rubbers, etc are dependent upon what one can scrounge, so your boat may differ in these details from ours. All that need be said is: get *sound* materials, but not necessarily the most expensive. This goes for fastenings too: use brass screws, etc. Mild steel screws are a bad economy. As for adhesives, we used S.P. Systems two-part epoxy glue. You may well go on to build a larger and more complex boat later on, so it is worth getting used to working with epoxy glue. Properly used, in accordance with the maker's instructions, and following the basic health and safety precautions, you will achieve gratifying results and an insight into the many uses to which these adhesives can be put.

Plan 5.2 Hull section and plan.

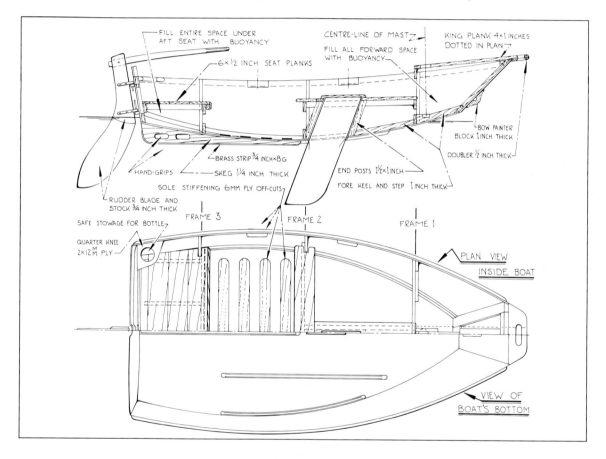

Unlike the first two boats in this book, *Punto* requires a strong building base on which to set up the frames. This ladder-like structure is detailed in the set of plans. What is needed is the means to set up frames precise distances apart. *Punto* is only 9 ft 6 in overall, but are you going to stop there? You've already flicked through the pages of this book before getting this far. Maybe you have at the back of your mind the thought that

Kilda or *Beachboat* could be a project at a future date. It will be no more trouble, and little extra expense, to make up a building base that will take a larger boat. The requirements are the same: the base must be strong, rigid, also 'squared' fore-and aft and athwartships. There is no need to buy new timber for the building base; in fact recycled, seasoned timber is often much better. Typical timber dimensions for a building base are given in the chapter on *Kilda*.

Photo 5.2 Frames fixed to cross pieces which are firmly screwed or bolted to the building base. Great care is needed to make sure each frame is plumb upright exactly on the centre-line, and not twisted so that one side is slightly further forward than the other.

Before starting construction, look and look again at the plans with their instructions. Get a clear picture in your mind of the stages of construction and what each will involve in materials, equipment and labour.

The operational procedure for *Punto* is as follows:

1. Make up frames and transom frames.
2. Set up frames on the building base and align correctly.
3. Fit and fasten chines.
4. Bevel frames and chines.
5. Plank the sides, starting with the top (sheer) plank.
6. Plank the bottom, using the single sheet of plywood.
7. Fit transom boards to their frames.
8. Fit skeg and runners.
9. Turn over.
10. Fit dagger-board case (in sailing version) and keelsons.
11. Fit thwarts, bottom doublers, bow beak and other details.
12. Fit gunwhale rubbers.
13. Paint and varnish.
14. For the sailing version, make dagger-board, rudder, spars, etc.

The set of plans (for availability see the address at the end of the chapter) includes full-scale drawings of the frames as they should be built and marked. Follow these very accurately, as they are the basis of a rigid and balanced boat. You will note that the frames extend above the level of the gunwhale to a common datum level. The boat is built upside down and this datum level is the level of the top of the building base.

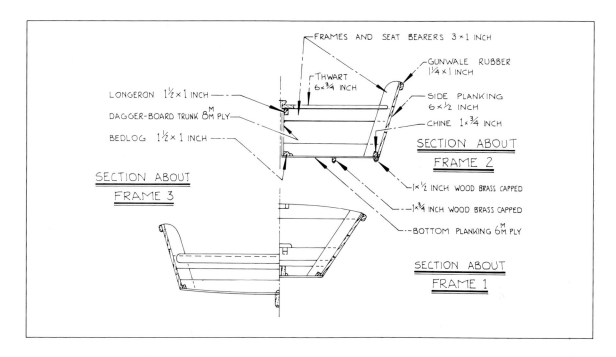

FRAMES AND SEAT BEARERS 3×1 INCH

THWART 6×¾ INCH

LONGERON 1½×1 INCH

DAGGER-BOARD TRUNK 8M PLY

BEDLOG 1½×1 INCH

GUNWALE RUBBER 1¼×1 INCH

SIDE PLANKING 6×½ INCH

CHINE 1×¾ INCH

SECTION ABOUT FRAME 2

SECTION ABOUT FRAME 3

1×½ INCH WOOD BRASS CAPPED

1×¾ INCH WOOD BRASS CAPPED

BOTTOM PLANKING 6M PLY

SECTION ABOUT FRAME 1

Plan 5.3 Frame sections.

Some people may be inclined to 'halve' the joints of bottom and side frames. This is not necessary, but if you have the experience to do a neat and strong job there is nothing to stop you.

The spacing of the frames is irregular. It is important to get these spacings right: measure and remeasure. If the building base sides are absolutely parallel and in a straight line, you can use a big square to square across. Even then, I would be inclined to double-check by using a steel tape from a centre-line point at one end of the building base sides, to make sure that the frame marks are equidistant each side.

Photo 5.2 shows how the frames are fitted to the cross pieces on the building base. You will note that at this stage the transom frames are open. This facilitates the fitting of the side planks and bottom. Use a piece of spare timber along the centre of the bottom of the boat to ensure the frames do not move while you fix the chines in place and bevel the frames.

Bevelling is a bug-bear to many people. It need not be. Arm yourself with a lath of timber (say 2 in × ¼ in) that will extend over at least *three* of the frames and a really sharp block plane. Lay the lath over the frames and then gently plane each frame edge until the lath lies sweetly and fair across them. Do this for both sides and bottom, and include the chines in this fairing process.

Planking commences from the top (sheer) strake, ie the bottom plank as you see it on the inverted boat. This requires no shaping, as it is so designed that it will take up the correct curve of the sheer. The second

81

Photo 5.3 Bow transom frame held by a cross-piece sloped back at the correct angle and firmly held by screws into the building base. The diagonal strut holds the frame at the precise angle shown on the plans.

Photo 5.4 Strips of wood clamped outside and inside the planking to keep the second plank in line while the glue sets. The strips have polythene sheet under them to prevent them sticking to the planks.

plank also requires no shaping; and the real bottom plank only requires to be shaped *after* fitting to take up the curve of the chine. Plank up in pairs: put on both sheer planks, then both middle planks and finally both bottom planks, so as to equalise the strain on each side of the boat framing. Trim the plank ends to be flush with the faces of the transom frames.

When laying the bottom ply, mark a centre-line down the length of the ply sheet on the inside and outside. If the inside is to be varnished this should be made the best side. Ensure that this line goes on the centre-line of the frames. Mark the outside edge of the ply outside the chines with a pencil and cut full to allow for fine trimming (with your block plane) when the ply is finally fixed.

Photo 5.5 Each plank is edge-glued to the next. Countersunk screws hold the ends to the transom frames. When the glue has set the excess length is cut off.

Photo 5.6 Ply being glued to the transom frame, before the aft seat is fitted. Lots of clamps are used, with wooden pads with polythene underneath to prevent damage or sticking to the frame.

With all the planking it is a good tip to mark on the inside where all the frames will abut, and then to drill pilot holes in preparation for drilling and countersinking the fastening holes. Remove any dust or drill chippings before applying the epoxy. The same applies to the fittings and fixing of the transom coverings, which should be fitted at this stage.

The skeg and main fore-and-aft bottom rubbers are screwed on from the inside of the hull. Mark their locations and drill pilot holes as with the planking. The smaller rubbers on the chines are screwed on from the outside into the chines.

Photo 5.7 Bottom rubbers and skeg to protect the ply bottom, especially important when hauling the boat up a rough beach. The skeg hand-holes are for lifting the boat, tying her down or for holding onto in an emergency afloat.

When turning the boat over, unscrew the hull from the building base. When all is ready, invite a few friends to come and have a beer or two and look at the boat. You will be amazed how quickly and easily the boat will be turned over, and if you play it correctly all you will have to do is stand by and give instructions!

If you are building the sailing version, now is the time to make and fit the dagger-board case and the keelsons. Make up each dagger-board case side with its bedlog (lower stiffener), then attach the end posts to one side. At this point coat the *insides* with epoxy, as you will never get another chance to do this so thoroughly. Assemble the second side to the end posts, staggering the screws so that they don't foul each other as they come in from opposite sides. Trim any excess ply, etc. There is a slight 'rocker' to the bottom, so you will need to plane the bedlogs to accomodate this. Use a good bedding compound and screw through from the outside. Do the same for the keelsons.

The thwarts, bow beak, doublers, etc are shown on plans 5.2 and 5.3. The quarter-knees are made up from layers of ply offcuts glued together

Photo 5.8 Dagger-board case must be well secured against movement athwartships and fore-and-aft. The case is assembled and glued up complete, before being fitted to the boat.

Photo 5.9 Beak helps to keep water out of the boat in rough conditions and hand-hole is useful for lashing the boat down or carrying her. A wood or PVC foredeck can be fitted and this bow area should be filled with buoyancy.

and then cut to shape. The hole takes a milk bottle (or a litre wine bottle) with ease and avoids spilling the contents in the bilge!

The gunwhale rubbers are best made up of three laminates of some hardwood such as mahogany. The boat itself makes the best former for gluing up. Separate the rubber from the hull with some plastic sheet so that the rubber does not stick to the hull prematurely! Plane to shape as shown when it is set hard, and fix to the hull with screws from the inside. It is debatable whether one should also glue the rubber to the hull. Some people never do this because the rubber will get chafed and damaged, since that is its purpose, and will be more easily replaced if not glued in place. Please yourself!

As to the finish, we painted the boat both inside and out, and only varnished the thwarts and gunwhale rubbers because they were both of attractive mahogany!

If you are building the sailing model, the plans and instructions give you all the information for making the dagger-board, rudder and spars, as well as details of the sail and running rigging.

Why the name 'Punto'? Well, in Australia, where I lived for many years, any pram-type dinghy is always referred to as a 'punt' or 'punto'; it seemed an appropriate name.'

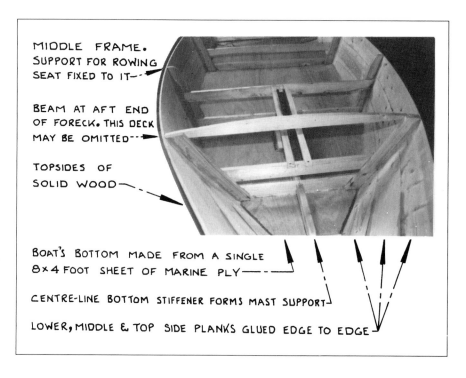

MIDDLE FRAME.
SUPPORT FOR ROWING
SEAT FIXED TO IT

BEAM AT AFT END
OF FORECK. THIS DECK
MAY BE OMITTED

TOPSIDES OF
SOLID WOOD

BOAT'S BOTTOM MADE FROM A SINGLE
8×4 FOOT SHEET OF MARINE PLY

CENTRE-LINE BOTTOM STIFFENER FORMS MAST SUPPORT

LOWER, MIDDLE & TOP SIDE PLANKS GLUED EDGE TO EDGE

AUTHORS' NOTE The prototype was made with $\frac{3}{8}$ in thick side planks and no chines. Along the join edges of the bottom and lowest planks, inside and out, 3 in glassfibre tape was applied using epoxy resin. Also the frames were not bevelled, though the transom edges were.

Detailed plans, including full-size sections for making frames, and instructions may be obtained from David Ryder-Turner, Dunard Cottage, Station Road, Rhu, Dunbartonshire, Scotland, G84 8LW. Price, including packing and postage, £37.00.

SOLID WOOD KNEES ARE SCREWED
AND GLUED TO UNDER-SIDE OF
BEAM ALSO TO AFT FACE OF FRAME

KING PLANK GOES FROM
BEAM TO RECESS IN TOP
FRAME PIECE OF BOW
TRANSOM

DARK LINE IS FIBRE-
GLASS TAPE EPOXY
GLUED TO TOPSIDES
AND BOTTOM PLY

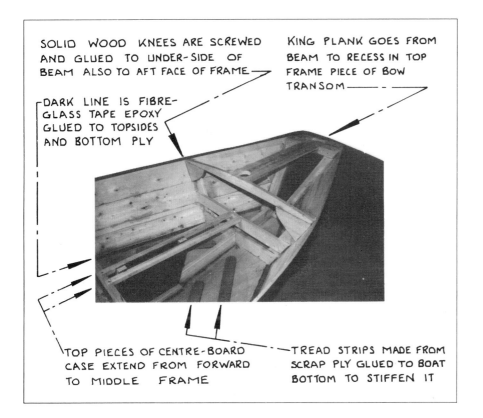

TOP PIECES OF CENTRE-BOARD
CASE EXTEND FROM FORWARD
TO MIDDLE FRAME

TREAD STRIPS MADE FROM
SCRAP PLY GLUED TO BOAT
BOTTOM TO STIFFEN IT

CHAPTER 6
Beachboat 14 feet overall

Beachboat is a una-rig planing dinghy for one or two people. She is light and can be rigged, launched and retrieved by one person. She has a sparkling performance and is extremely fast in a good sailing breeze, whilst being easily sailed with her una-rig. She can be built by a reasonably competent amateur woodworker with the usual hand tools and home workshop. The combination of round bilge forward and a chine aft is not only easy to construct, but is a significant factor in her performance.

Beachboat *was designed and built by a friend of ours, David Ryder-Turner, while he was living in Australia. In this chapter he describes the concept of this attractive craft and outlines the method of construction.*

'What do you sail when you are getting too old and fat to hike out on the end of the sliding seat of a 10-Square-Metre Canoe? You want the performance without the demands on agility and strength. I was living in Adelaide, South Australia, where there are endless sandy beaches but in those days an inadequate number of launching ramps.

Thus the boat that I should have had to be light enough to tow behind a small car and suitable for launching from beaches, if possible single-handed. So the concept of a light, fast and easily handled craft came into being. The boat had to be capable of carrying two adults or an adult and two children. Naturally one expected the performance to be less sparkling with the additional weight, but not too much less.

Lightness and strength is the key to this design. The relatively small cockpit space and the large amount of decking make for a construction that is inherently strong – like *Cove Boat* and *Longa* – without the need for a lot of frames.

Apart from its singular purpose, the most significant feature of this design is the 'disappearing' chine. There is little doubt that, for planing purposes, a chine hull is the best; but for windward work it is not always

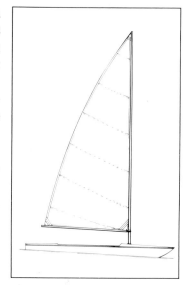

Plan 6.1 Sail plan.

Plan 6.2 Hull lines.

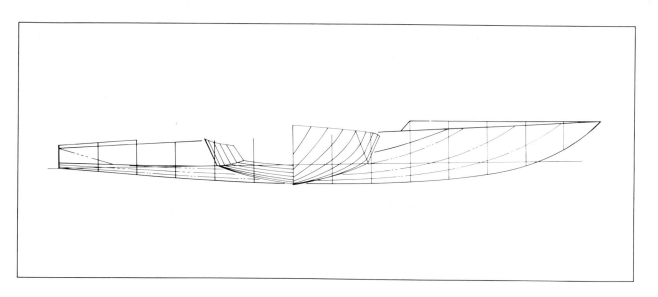

the more efficient: one wants a round-bilge configuration for this. Round-bilge construction is rather daunting for the inexperienced builder, involving either carvel, clinker (lapstrake) or cold-moulded techniques.

Kilda is an excellent example of how a round bilge can be achieved with a minimum of planks on a lapstrake hull. *Beachboat*, in contrast, is built using large sheets of ply bent in a special way. A sheet of plywood (or even paper) cannot be bent in two directions at once, though one can achieve slight double curvatures as in *Punto*. By using the geometrical construction called 'conical projection' it is possible to coax large sheets of ply into a round-bilge form.

It works like this: take a piece of paper and form it into a cone; clip or stick it so that it holds the shape. Now lay a ruler on a line from the apex to the base; it is a straight line. Lay the rule at an *angle*, and the line is curved; what is more, the line at a right angle to it is curved in the other direction. It would seem, then, that plywood *can* form a complex curved surface.

This is the basis of the 'conical projection which enables a hull to be round-bilge forward and chined aft. The bottom plank meets the topside plank at the aft end of the boat at a marked angle, forming the chine. Working forward from the transom, the bottom plank takes up an increasingly greater curvature from keel to topside, until the bottom plank goes right up the sheer line and the chine disappears. Plan 6.2 shows this sufficiently well for the form to be clear. There is another advantage to this shape because, in spite of the light scantling of the

Plan 6.3 Hull section and plan.

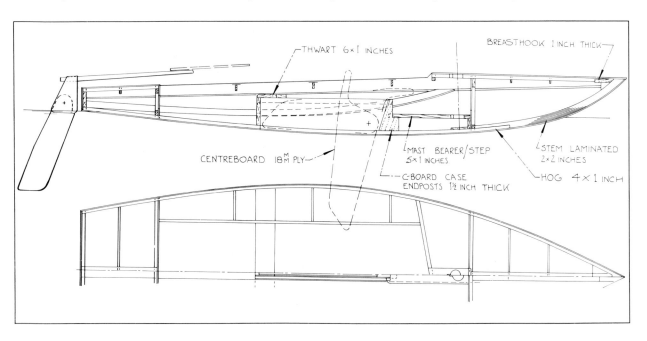

plywood (6 mm), the curving sections give it increasing strength just where needed. It is a form of stressed-skin construction. I have used this form on other craft: my last International 10-Square-Metre Canoe was made in this way.

The two bulkheads – one at each end of the cockpit – and the transom are the only permanent frames, and are made up of light timber covered by 6 mm plywood. There are also a further four building moulds. These are made of scrap timber, or 3 in × 1 in pine, that can be broken up after they have fulfilled their function. The stem is laminated upon a former, set up on a 'scrieve-board' which is just a large piece of flat wood on which the frames, etc are marked out full-size. The scrieve-board for this boat was a piece of 1 in chipboard, 6 ft × 3 ft. On it were drawn the sections of the bulkheads and moulds. So, too, was the stem. After the frames/moulds had been fabricated (and checked), we set up 2 in pieces of angle iron on the inside of the curve of the stem. With these securely screwed to the scrieve-board, we were able to bend the $\frac{1}{8}$ in laminates to the correct curve, one after the other, up to the desired depth of the stem.

Photo 6.2 *Beachboat* is built upside-down on a building base which gives firm support to the frames. Plenty of working space is needed all round.

Beachboat is built upside down and the frames and moulds are set up in the same manner as for *Punto*. The curved stem has to be fixed temporarily at its top to a strong board set athwart the building base and at its bottom end to the first mould.

The keel, a piece of Oregon pine, is fitted permanently to the two bulkheads and transom and stem; but only temporary screws hold it to the moulds, which are withdrawn when the hull is lifted off the stocks and turned the right way for finishing. Gunwhales and chines are glued and screwed permanently to the bulkheads and transom, but only tempor-

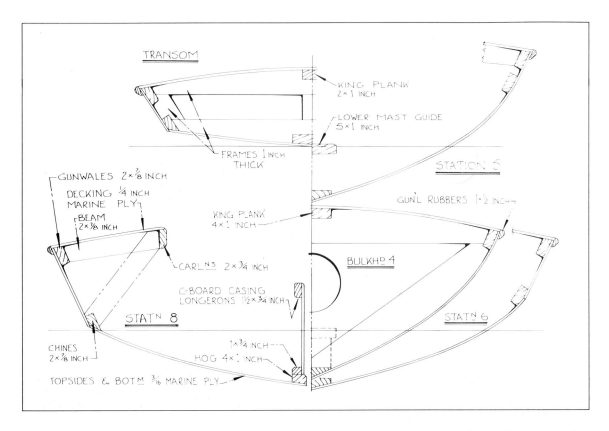

TRANSOM

KING PLANK
2 × 1 INCH

LOWER MAST GUIDE
5 × 1 INCH

FRAMES 1 INCH
THICK

STATION 5

GUNWALES 2 × 7/8 INCH

DECKING 1/4 INCH
MARINE PLY

GUN'L RUBBERS 1 1/2 INCH

BEAM
2 × 7/8 INCH

KING PLANK
4 × 1 INCH

CARL'NS 2 × 3/4 INCH

BULKHD 4

C-BOARD CASING
LONGERONS 1 1/2 × 3/4 INCH

STAT'N 8

STAT'N 6

CHINES
2 × 7/8 INCH

1 × 3/4 INCH

HOG 4 × 1 INCH

TOPSIDES & BOT'M 3/16 MARINE PLY

Plan 6.4 Station sections.

arily to the moulds. Because they are the only other pieces running lengthwise in the boat, apart from gunwhales and keel, the chines have to be of fairly heavy scantling: $1\frac{1}{2}$ in $\times$ $\frac{3}{4}$ in. They take up a double curve at their fore end which does take some small persuasion. Unless you have a steam-box, which we hadn't, you will find that wrapping the fore end of the chines in sacking or cloth, and then soaking these with hot water, makes the timber pliable enough for the chines to be clamped in place and left for 24 hours, before removing and preparing for final fitting. The timber retains the curvature and fits easily in place for gluing and screwing.

The planking is relatively simple: for each side two 8 ft × 4 ft marine ply panels are scarfed end-to-end, giving a single panel of 15 ft 9 in × 4 ft. I got the suppliers to do this, but now feel confident, some boats later, that I can do the scarfing myself. Like so many of the processes in small boat building, patience, accuracy and careful planning make it possible to undertake jobs you might think are beyond you. Having someone on hand who has a bit more experience is a great boost to your confidence.

Because the bottom plank is such a strange shape, and it is difficult to handle the 15 ft 9 in long sheet uncut, it is worth making a pattern of this plank. The pattern can be made from any sufficiently stiff material. I used two large sheets of cardboard glued and stapled together, but a friend, for a similar boat, used a large sheet of heavy-gauge polythene sheeting. In retrospect, I think I like his way the better. You will need to 'offer up' and test this plank a few times, until you get it right, but you will be surprised how well it does take up the curvature forward. One thing you *will* need is a number of G-clamps, which can be borrowed, bought or hired.

Photo 6.3 Hull with bottom ply in position and side pieces about to follow. Note the 'disappearing' chine which gives the effect of round bilge sections forward.

When planking is complete turn the boat over, but leave the moulds in place until you have laminated the external gunwhale rubber. This should be done *before* you put the deck on, for ease of clamping.

This boat has extensive decking, but there are a number of items that must be frabricated and fitted before you deck the craft. The sequence of operation is detailed in the instructions that go with the set of plans.

Unlike the other craft in this book, *Beachboat* has a centre-board that is pivoted on a pin. The board is moved up and down without the use of a tackle. What holds the board in one position is a piece of split tubing screwed to its aft edge. When the screws are tightened they spread the tubing so that it presses firmly against the inside of the centre-board trunk.

Originally I was going to fabricate a spruce mast, but when I built *Beachboat*, I was able to get a metal spar without fittings similar to that used on a Laser dinghy, that did the job perfectly. As the sailplan shows, this is a very simple rig with plenty of opportunity for 'tweaking' and fine-tuning. At one time I did consider a loose-footed sail, but decided against it. One would have had to have a goose-neck fitting instead of the

Photo 6.4 Before taking the boat off the building base, the bottom is rubbed well down and given all but the final coat or two of varnish or paint. The area where the rubber will be glued to the gunwale is left bare.

Photo 6.5 Boat is carefully blocked up after she has been turned over, so that the hull is firmly supported while completion work goes ahead. Before the deck goes on, the inside is painted or varnished.

standard jaws, and this seemed more of a fiddle than slipping the foot of the sail along the boom slot. The latter also made for easier tensioning of the foot.

So simple is the launching and rigging of this craft that the time it took for the trailer to be rolled down the beach, the craft unloaded, rigged and lifted (or dragged!) to the water was only 7 minutes.

I spent some time looking for the best trailer. Finally I got one with a bow chock that swivelled, so all one had to do was unlash the boat, pick up the stern and swivel the boat through 90°. One can then lift the bow off easily, and all is ready for rigging.

We had a lot of fun with this boat and when I left South Australia, I gave her to a friend whose children still get a huge amount of enjoyment from her. She has been trailed literally thousands of miles.'

A complete set of plans and instructions, including full-size sections, may be obtained from David Ryder-Turner, Dunard Cottage, Station Road, Rhu, Dunbartonshire, Scotland, G84 8LW. Price, including packing and postage, £37.00.

CHAPTER 7
Spars

The cheapest way to get a complete rig is to buy a second-hand one. This is done by asking friends if they know anyone who is upgrading his boat, or has old spars and sails lying in his loft or garage. The second line of inquiry is through the local sailing club. A notice on the board is quite likely to produce results especially if a local class has changed from wood to alloy spars. In three years of boatbuilding together the authors came across lots of old but usable masts, booms and sails. Some were offered free, some for nothing more than a donation to the Royal National Lifeboat Institution.

If no local spars can be found, try a 'wanted' advertisement in the classified columns of a yachting magazine which specialises in small craft. Some magazines have classified sections dealing with spars and sails.

Plenty of sellers have no idea what price to ask. Others accept that it is a buyer's market. If in doubt, offer between one quarter and one eighth of the new value, according to condition. These figures have been established by practice, but good old-fashioned bargaining may be needed.

If sails and spars are bought from different sources they may not mate together well. In general it is best to buy the spars first; they tend to be the most difficult to find, especially masts. Booms are easy to make and require little in the way of materials or skill. Once a mast has been bought the assembly of a complete rig tends to be fairly easy. Sails can sometimes be bought second-hand from sail-makers. Occasionally a mainsail will need different slides or a change of luff-rope to fit the mast or boom.

Spars bought second-hand may be of wood or alloy. In the same way, spars made by an amateur can be of these materials. In yachting magazines there are advertisements for mast kits. These are intended for amateurs, and include aluminium tubes and the fittings to go with them. Assembly does not take much time or skill. Alternatively a boat builder can buy alloy tubes and make up his own spars using the 'long-wire' method described on page 398 of the *Ian Nicolson Omnibus* published by Ashford Press.

Another way to get low-priced spars is to have them made of wood by a boat yard or even by an intelligent and skilled joiner. If the owner makes and fixes the fittings, and does all the varnishing, there will be a useful cash saving. Even better, the amateur can make up his own wood spars.

The dimensions of the spars for some of the boats in this book are given in detail. To make spars a flat work-bench the full length of the mast is an enormous asset. Failing this, a work-bench which is more than a third the length of the longest spar is about the minimum, though we have worked on flat floors, in garages . . . anywhere clean, dry and free from draughts. A firm method of holding the length of wood being turned into a spar is essential, as there is a lot of cutting and planing to do. A pair of Black and Decker Workmate benches, or better still three of them, can be used. To avoid buying a batch of these useful benches, cultivate the sensible sort of friend who will lend his Workmate.

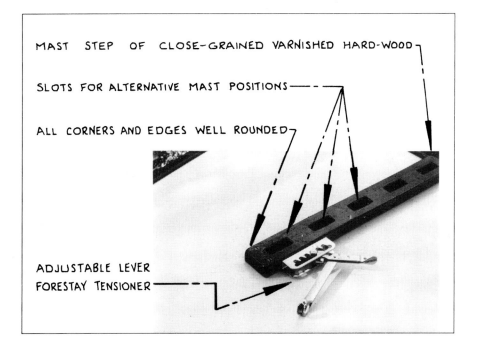

MAST STEP OF CLOSE-GRAINED VARNISHED HARD-WOOD

SLOTS FOR ALTERNATIVE MAST POSITIONS

ALL CORNERS AND EDGES WELL ROUNDED

ADJUSTABLE LEVER
FORESTAY TENSIONER

In this book the spars drawn out are all of solid wood. To save wood, and to reduce the weight of the spars, hollow masts and booms may be made. The principle is simple; each spar is just a long thin box of wood. Typically the wall thickness of the spar will be one quarter of the diameter. So if a mast is being made up with a finished athwartships diameter of 2 in, and a fore-and-aft diameter of 3 in, the side walls would be $\frac{1}{2}$ in thick, and the fore-and-aft ones $\frac{3}{4}$ in thick.

The quality of the wood must be excellent, and if there are any knots they must be right at the bottom end of the mast, or near the outer ends of the boom. Even then these knots must be less than $\frac{1}{4}$ in across and tight in the wood. The spars are glued with epoxy resin, and clamped together at about 8 in intervals, with long wood packing pieces under the clamp jaws to spread the pressure widely. To save using so many clamps some amateurs use ropes wound round the spars, with lots of wedges driven in. These apply pressure to hold the staves together while the glue sets.

To ensure that the mast finishes up absolutely straight, the gluing up must be done with the mast lying on a perfectly level surface. This may be hard to find, and clever builders accept this. They select a surface which has a slight curvature and make up the mast so that it bends back at the top. Since most sailing is done with some backward bend in the mast, this permanent curvature is usually acceptable.

When the spar has been glued up, its edges are planed round. A track is screwed on the aft side of the mast to take the mainsail, or a luff groove may be made, if the builder's skill and patience extend that far.

CHAPTER 8
Safety

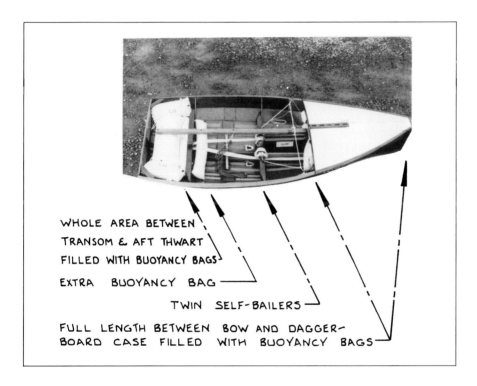

WHOLE AREA BETWEEN
TRANSOM & AFT THWART
FILLED WITH BUOYANCY BAGS

EXTRA BUOYANCY BAG

TWIN SELF-BAILERS

FULL LENGTH BETWEEN BOW AND DAGGER-
BOARD CASE FILLED WITH BUOYANCY BAGS

What follows may sound rather dramatic but we make no apology for including it and recommend all readers to study it carefully.

▶THE CREW

When going afloat in any small boat, even in the most sheltered place, it is vital for each person to wear a life-jacket or a buoyancy aid. And there is a difference between the two. A proper life-jacket floats the wearer high in the water with the head tilted back. It provides full support in case of injury or loss of consciousness. A buoyancy aid is what it says: an *aid*. It should support you in normal sailing clothes without the need to swim or assist yourself. With young children and non-swimmers a life-jacket is needed. Buy a product that meets your national standards.

It is important to wear warm clothing. It is almost invariably colder on the water than on land so do not be deceived by conditions on shore. It is better to put on too much clothing to start with. If you are cold on the water, this leads to diminished efficiency and strength and that is when mistakes are made. A wet-suit is advisable with performance dinghies and makes launching of any dinghy easier and more comfortable. Wet-suit gloves and hood or a woolly hat are also a good idea.

▶ THE BOAT

Adequate buoyancy is essential. Some fully or partially decked dinghies like *Cove Boat*, *Longa* or *Beachboat* have contained air spaces which make them buoyant. Even so it is worth considering filling these spaces with buoyant material. Other dinghies such as *Punto* and *Kilda* do not have any sealed air spaces and therefore buoyancy bags or material must be fitted. The photograph at the beginning of this chapter shows the location of buoyancy bags fore and aft in *Kilda*, and the chapter on *Kilda* gives details of the size and number of buoyancy bags we have fitted for a dinghy of this size. In the event of a capsize it is important to have enough buoyancy to support the whole crew and make the boat float high enough in the water, so that when she is righted it is possible to get sailing again quickly. This means that the top of the dagger-board case must be about 5 in above water level.

Buoyancy bags exert a considerable strain on their fastenings when immersed, so ensure that they are well secured. We also feel that it is preferable to achieve the necessary buoyancy with a number of smaller bags rather than just a few large ones, because the effect of a bag being damaged is less severe.

Other essential equipment to carry on board includes a paddle or paddles, hand bailers and a set of flares, all of which should be accessible and attached to the boat. Make sure all crew members are familiar with the instructions for the use of the flares.

You should be able to tow your boat with another and the only way to do this is to have an adequate mooring cleat (see plan 3.12).

▶ SAFE CONDUCT

If you are new to sailing, join a course at an officially approved sailing school or gain some experience with an experienced and knowledge-able sailor. Learn the procedure for righting a capsized dinghy. Learn the rules for navigation at sea (ie who has the right of way, etc) and also learn any local harbour regulations that may apply.

Listen to the weather forecast for your area and do not venture onto the water in unsuitable conditions, bearing in mind both your own and your crew's ability. If you are sailing in an unfamiliar area try to acquire some local knowledge before going afloat and if sailing on the sea get tidal charts.

CONVERSION TABLE

INCHES	MILLIMETRES	FEET	METRES
$\frac{1}{16}$	1.6	1	0.305
$\frac{1}{8}$	3.2	2	0.610
$\frac{1}{4}$	6.4	3	0.914
$\frac{3}{8}$	9.5	4	1.219
$\frac{1}{2}$	12.7	5	1.524
$\frac{3}{4}$	19.1	6	1.829
1	25.4	7	2.134
2	50.8	8	2.438
3	76.2	9	2.743
4	101.6	10	3.048
5	127.0	11	3.353
6	152.4	12	3.658
7	177.8	13	3.962
8	203.2	14	4.267
9	228.6		
10	254.0		
11	279.4		
12	304.8		